Denny's Arbor Vitae

DENNY'S ARBOR VITAE
Poetic Memoirs

A Collection of Poems by

TIMOTHY ROBBINS

Adelaide Books
New York / Lisbon

2017

DENNY'S ARBOR VITAE / Poetic Memoirs
A Collection of Poems
By Timothy Robbins

Copyright © 2017 By Timothy Robbins
Illustrations Copyright © 2017 ~By Timothy Robbins

Published by Adelaide Books, New York / Lisbon
An imprint of the Istina Group DBA
adelaidebooks.org

Editor-in-Chief
Stevan V. Nikolic

Cover Image: Timothy Robbins
Cover Design & Book Formatting: Istina Group DBA

All rights reserved. No part of this book may be reproduced in any manner whatsoever without written permission from the author except in the case of brief quotations embodied in critical articles and reviews.

For any information, please address Adelaide Books
at info@adelaidebooks.org

ISBN13: 978-0-9992148-3-1
ISBN10: 0-9992148-3-7

Printed in the United States of America

For David and Jeff.
Poetry could have no finer friends and neither could I.

Self-portrait with Guitar

Contents

FAMILY'S LONG MEGAPHONE

- *15* Infancy of Recording
- *17* Isometrics
- *19* Rollin (sometimes Roland) Eugene Robbins
- *21* It
- *23* The Night Mom Chased a Thief
- *26* Bildungsroman
- *27* Bill
- *28* The Brush
- *29* Communion
- *30* Cousins
- *32* Experimental Likeness
- *35* The Filling
- *38* Father and Son at Melody Mart
- *41* Haines City
- *42* Breaking the Diaries
- *45* Weddings
- *47* Laguna Beach
- *49* Led by the Nose

Loner *51*
Mine *54*
Nannie *55*
To the Nursery with Dad *58*
Western *59*
Wynwood Walls *60*
Raphael *61*
Foundation *63*
Trails *64*

NARCISSUS POETICUS

Night Visitors *67*
Failure of a Miraculous Birthday *69*
Bowing *70*
Chuang Tzu's Butterfly *71*
The Cut *73*
Diagnosed *74*
Fault Lines *76*
Abandoned Thoughts *77*
Advice *78*
Assets *79*
Astrology *80*
At Twelve *82*
Atripla *83*
Ballet *85*
Sal Mineo *86*

87   Christ
89   Cornrows
90   The Ghost of the Rose
92   Gita Raga Rag
94   Lay of the Land
97   Mercy
98   One Gate into the City
100   Potential
102   Residuals
105   Tight Places

COMMON LAW

109   Passover
110   How You Came to Me
111   Couvre-Feu
113   The Prayer
115   Marriage
116   Timber
117   You are Sitting at the Table
120   Another Flag
121   At Home
122   How to Break the News to the Nguyens
123   Bird
124   Dressed Up
126   The Treader
127   Fuller Street Daruma

Hard Reach *129*
In the Air *130*
My Two Marriages *131*
No Day at the Beach *133*
Ode to a Boy from Hanoi *134*
Chicagos (for Mike) *136*
Waiters *137*
For Mike *138*
Thanksgiving in Chicago *139*
Today *141*
Stuck *143*

PASSENGERS

Letter to Gregg *146*
The Way of Tim Ash *148*
Tannenbaum *150*
Marc *152*
Essay *155*
What We Know *156*
Nostalgia *157*
Chantel Two Days Before Halloween *158*
Charla and the Traveler *159*
Engagement *161*
The Women *163*
Train *166*
Strasbourg Gang *169*

171   Sandra's Poem
172   The Portrait
173   The Messenger
175   Kotaro
177   Kazu
178   John
180   Joel
182   Harry's Poem
185   The Brothers
187   For Nell
188   Farewell

191   Publishing credits
195   About the Author

"Miracle of the Fishes"

Family's Long Megaphone

Infancy of Recording

The stylus etches arbitrary sound, not
too shallow, not too deep,
cutting impressionable tinfoil, lead or wax.
A needle is set into the groove and rides the
cylinder round and round just as we
ride the calendar. I was
receptive to every word said, read or
sung to me. I learned to play back every
hymn I heard, lowering the needle into the
grooves of my young brain in the infancy
of recording. Especially songs my
grandmother sang — most of them
about the land she came from, places my
grandfather took her, the place where she
would follow him some day.
In 1930 they drove to Frankfort to get the
license and since they were there, married
in the fancy sanctuary instead of the log
church on Back Creek. He borrowed
the only car in the county, left
both mothers behind. There was
barely room for the couple and the
patriarchs to ride. She wore her best blue
Sunday dress (all she could afford).
There was nothing but the family
Bible to record the momentous event.
Record, film or photograph
were beyond the reach of folks who

didn't have the money to buy
clothes that would be worn just once
or take a honeymoon that was more
than dancing on the cold dirt floor where
they went to housekeeping.
I'm listening to "My Old Kentucky Home"
on a wax cylinder — voices from 1905
etched warm and scratchy with
attention to diction long since lost and
harmonies tight as cornhusks. The cylinder,
more expensive than a flat disc, affords
greater dynamic range of hill
and dale geometry — rather like
the Blue Grass State itself. The sound
is traced by a pantograph —
a marriage of pens in which one tries to
imitate the dance of its partner but always
deviates further and further
till it reaches the last generation,
the process destroying
the progenitor. The truth is amplified
by a cone attached to a diaphragm.
I never lived in Kentucky.
Neither did Stephen Foster.
But if technology lets me join in with the
Edison Male Quartet a century after they
gathered around that long megaphone,
singing, "Weep no more, my lady, weep no
more today," who's to say I
won't be heard?

Denny's Arbor Vitae

Isometrics

I've found him again after all these years,
the man in the isometrics book.
My father was just out of school with a
job in the ball bearing plant,
a pretty young wife with cat's eye glasses
and a drawerful of gauzy headscarfs,
and outside the trailer, a new well that
set them back two hundred dollars.
I've studied the wedding photos, how the
tux made him look like a fancy
scarecrow. I've heard about the first time
my mother burst through the farmhouse
door where her mother was cranking
sopping clothes through a wringer. "I've
got a date with Johnny Robbins,"
she announced. "That skinny little
thing?" her mother snorted.

Today after all these years I've found it
again — my father's isometrics book.
The miracle that it still exists makes me
believe that I, the child exploring the
lower bookshelves, still exist too.

There you stand in nothing but tight
black trunks like a halter top bind-
ing your hips. You turn this way and that
in your strangely sparse universe.
Nothing but a wall for you to push against

and a single straight-back chair
from which you levitate promising some
unnamed sensation that marries
thrill and balance. A rod you grip in your
luminous knuckles is attached to
an elastic cord (the meaning entirely
escaped me). Now I know it's body
oil that makes your young muscles gleam.
Then it was the muscles themselves
that glowed like firefly abdomens in a
glass jar by my bed.

Now I see each photo is an arrested
movement, each movement, an
unfulfilled yearning for sport. gathering
strength for a game that will never
be played. Here is the Platonic ideal of the
javelin throw, the discus hurl, the
catcher's expectant crouch, the pitcher's
sweet release.

How lonely you are! Like an only child.
There is nobody else in your Spartan
room though there is a door in some of
the figures and a strip of wainscoting
lit by the bulbs of your biceps and calves.

All these years I've been trying to
come through that door, to relieve your
stoic look, relieving no one but myself.

Denny's Arbor Vitae

Rollin (sometimes Roland) Eugene Robbins

A tool and dye maker, you earned enough to
fill your life with red: house, car, truck,

garage — all as furious as you were seemingly
calm. You painted crimson curtains on the

garage windows. You wanted to paint Grandma
but she wouldn't have it.

She hooked you as you hooked rugs, sitting
on the edge of the sofa with the blinds drawn

so no one would know you had a woman's
hobby. In retirement you drew on the only

paper you thought you deserved: 3x5 notepads
held together at the top by a bar of red glue.

A long-neglected kindergarten in your largest
unruled classroom .

There was always a river standing straight up
and you used to say to me, "I can't figure out

what's wrong with these rivers." If only they
had lain decent in bed like Grandma did, you

would have waited on them as you waited on
her. I think of the church bulletins you

rescued and stapled to the garage walls. And
a photo of you in your sailor suit,

your skinny wife at your side, your first child
(my father) in a sailor suit of his own. The

baby's saw more action than the man's. You'd
just finished boot camp when the

Enola Gay dropped her falling stars. I think
of the artist you never became, never even

suspected you wanted to be. I think of the
temper that supposedly evaporated like the

cologne in your collectible car bottles. I
wonder how these are related to the time you

and Dad nearly came to blows 'cause he took
away the plastic rifles you'd given us.

In the basement you cut our hair to the skin.

Denny's Arbor Vitae

It

The Last time you heard Ann Sothern sing
"The Last Time I saw Paris," flowers glinting
on her earlobes and her veil, made of and for
the silver screen, saddened you. The closest
you'll come to the City of Lights is the single
postcard from a college kid wafting like
summer wind through your factory thirty years
ago. It was the morning you woke and thought
*Everyone longs to be the gypsy bride or the
rogue who carries her off.* It was sitting on
the patio, snapping beans. A jet moved silently
across the sky and you absolutely could not
say why that silence woke your dormant
widowhood. The clever boy at your feet, so
clever you couldn't help worrying, suggested
it was because, in spite of the quiet, you knew
the jet was roaring. It was reading Huck Finn and
laughing helplessly. Reading Aristotle and
laughing, but that was probably mostly the
grass. There in the stacks more ruled by hush
than sanctuaries, laughing, not haughtily
but as a governess laughs at her willful charge.
It was standing with your wife of fifty years,
looking into the canyon, thinking *time is
doing the same to us only we are more easily
sculpted.* It was the last time you saw Back Creek.
The sons of the same old men chawed outside
the general store and your son-in-law tried, in

vain you knew, to capture them on his video-cam.
It was the first night we slept here. Our things
hadn't arrived yet. The bare floors held a thrill
of welcome, like a sufi's cleared out soul. It was
your garrulous but not usually eloquent parent
announcing *it's a privilege to be your mother.*
It was the first voice you heard as you recovered
from anesthesia: the mourning dove's query, the
embarrassed cough, campground dulcimers,
an irrepressible bottom smack, air struggling to
escape crêpe paper threaded through spokes,
whispers of all ages.

Denny's Arbor Vitae

The Night Mom Chased a Thief

I remembered a lot of things that night. How she made us
brushed denim leisure suits (like the Osmonds) specially

tailored for Sunday dinner at the Red Lobster Inn. How she
stood like a graduate in her choir robe singing solo at Sunrise

Services. Her Baptist upbringing. The root beer she wasn't
allowed to drink. The dances she could only imagine to Pat

Boone's voice on the radio. The movies her friends told her
about at the Damm Theater. (Grandma said no family had

any business flaunting such a name.) She only saw westerns
with her dad, projected at night on the side of a barn. The cowboys

only kissed with their fists, and when cards were dealt some
gambler always took a bullet in the head, proof that cards are

tools of the devil. I thought about her best friend Nancy and
their graduating class of sixteen — the number of the apostles

with the three Marys and Martha tossed in. The boys on the
basketball team with hair like the brush my dad used to buff our

Sunday shoes. Mom and Nancy in cat's eye glasses dreaming of
Natalie Wood. I wondered what secrets they swapped after dates,

lost or misplaced virginities, holding the darkest tears between
their legs. After graduation long hours candy-striping at the

local hospital watching new fathers humbled at the baby window,
bathing withered sexless relics at the Odd Fellows Home. I

thought of the souvenirs I found stashed in the closet. Tassels
long bereft of their rented mortar boards. Photos of a class trip

to Washington D.C.. Mom and Nancy looking like little kids
in their berths. Her report cards — grades my brother and I teased

her about. Much later, after my parents bought the store in one
olympian year she sold twenty pianos winning a vacation for

two in Jamaica. They came back with six bottles of rum that
lurked in the pantry for years, six forbidden fruit juices which my

grandmother never tired of railing against. I remembered how Dad
was always trying to teach her euchre She couldn't keep clubs

and spades straight much less master the ever-changing trump,
left and right bower. Dad would snap at her and she'd wind up

in the kitchen wiping her eyes on a dish rag. The store was closed
that night. She was working late on the books when the stillness

of her pencil scratching the paper was shattered by a shattering
of glass. The display window lay scattered on the floor. She ran

Denny's Arbor Vitae

out to the street and saw the thief go round the corner, a guitar
held high in each hand. She pursued him, shouting, into the alley

where two drunks who were stumbling out of the Dog House Tavern
tackled him. Those report cards, it turns out, were inadequate in

a whole other sense, giving no indication of her bravery or what
my friend Jeff calls her knack for always knowing the kind thing

to say. No prognostication of her victory over cancer. No sign that
on the night her gay son came out to her she would sit on the edge

of his bed and kissed his face in the dark.

Bildungsroman

Across the belly of Ohio, Indiana's stout brother,
I read *Beneath the Wheel* in the backseat of a gold
Impala. My own brother reads *The Autobiography
of Malcolm X*, my brother's whiteness as stark as
that single capital, the Roman numeral that crowns
Little the last of a long dynasty of secret rulers.
Grandmother, faithful to her late illiterate
husband, reads all signs out loud. That my mother
can drive ten hours straight only stopping for
burgers is a revelation. The steering wheel longs
for Dad's relaxed hold. This is the first of a short
cycle of trips in the course of which a pope will be
chosen and shot. Elvis will die and return for
an encore (bloated as a drowned white jumpsuit).
And I, with scant effort, will embrace my passionate
pity for the boy beneath the wheel.

Denny's Arbor Vitae

Bill

As long as he stayed on Sand Creek,
no one — not even himself — knew he was a bigot.
Lost opportunity protected him. No money to
supplement a tuba scholarship. Too late for the G.I.
Bill. Factory transfers went to slicker men.
Safe in the deep white of Decatur County,
he fished, hunted with a bow, mastered new
instruments culminating with the plectrum,
never suspecting the path that winds from plantation
to Chicago, from Funeral with Music to
the attentive ensembles of Original Jazz.

Even with her new knees Maggie has trouble
walking to the plot where graves blur smoothly
into cornfield. My first visitation, I'm glad
to see his skill with banjo, trombone,
tuba, guitar and organ carved into something
more durable than life. Musical notes above
his name. A floating treble clef with a single
sharp in the third space. In death as in life he plays
in a non-existent key.

The Brush

Eighteen, I sat on the floor. She brushed
my Lennon tribute. Sometimes even
braided it. Already she was shrinking,
thinning, the sectional sofa was
compressing her. She couldn't wield
the brush long. She whined admiringly,
"Mine was this strong when I was twenty."
Still she commended me to the barber
as if to confession. Fifty-two now, my
bangs are paltry. I bounce her brush in
my palm, feeling its heft and her lost vanity.
I should have brushed her hair — gently
to make her think I'm kinder than I am —
manfully to drive out prejudgments, hers
and mine — mechanically so she'd believe
I have stamina and could be repaired if I
broke down — playfully to remind her she'd
loved me when I was too young to play.
Thankfully. There are women who would
have given me blisters with this brush.

Denny's Arbor Vitae

Communion

I never tasted my mother's breasts.
Now it's too late.
First cancer came
then the poisons then the knives
then nausea then a pull that
left her slumped in the kitchen,
her bald head shining
for stools, coffee and strawberries.
Medicine and survival: a strange
bond between mother and
son when the others are still snoring
and we cross in the hall
on the way to our pills.
It's like being the only
Papists in a family of
Protestants, keeping each other
company, keeping faith
at the seven o'clock Mass.
We have this quiet inviolable
place just big enough for two.
A palmful of water
no more than a rescuer
would give victims who've been
parched so long, their rehydration
must be gradual.

Cousins

Now that your mother will sow
no more Crisco and sugar gardens,
force no more pastry-bag roses onto
snowy wedding cakes; now that she'll
stride no more fairways, swiping her
putter before her, as though witching
for bashful water or scaring up quail
for her husband; now that your father's
guffaw and cough, rifle and banjo stand
still as deer playing statue in the beam
you used to aim from your Mustang's
lowered window; now that my parents
have kept their cremation promise,
stranding though they meant to free
us; now that we've both lost our siblings
(your sister in Alabama, my brother in
California, both secure in bunker's of
flesh); now that the dogs have gone
to bark curfew in the hills of heaven
— Ernie, who pranced like young Isaac,
thrilled to precede you uphill, not despite
but because of the rifle you shouldered
— Jack, whom you fed to death — Yargo,
whom my mother leashed and led to the vet
though her mother stood at the backdoor
and said, "Stop, I don't care how many
messes I have to clean up." Now that this

Denny's Arbor Vitae

long procession has passed like a single lap
of the 500 race, it's you and me, face to face,
as we never expected. I remember panty
hose flattening your nose, forcing you to
breathe like a bulldog. Nine years, two feet,
a hundred pounds my senior, used to
toting a sousaphone, you had no trouble
swinging me over your shoulder, carrying
me (bouncing against your back) down to the
creek and dropping me in the water. I
remember the night you marveled at the
dinner table, "I've been all over this
country but I never seen no queers till
I came to this podunk village in Ohio."
You must have known I thought myself
a prodigy and you, a redneck. Now it's
you and me — and our mates. Your Debbie
(third wife of that name — it takes
perseverance to flush the right one) invites
my Mike and me for Thanksgiving. We talk
about the recession, the agony of Detroit, the
careless music of the past, Debbie's
favorite brother (he and his husband in
Las Vegas toasting the Cadillac they won
selling Mary Kay). We show each other our
shingles — yours on your back, mine on my
legs — and wonder at the patient infection
in our blood.

Experimental Likeness

Dramatis Personae. Not Divine, though my face apes his.
That one won't speak his lines till his face is painted with
reflections from gay stained glass — rouge and eye shadow

neither sweat nor tear can plow. This one wants to be graffiti,
mural or wrecking ball — whatever lends interest to a wall.
The forty-year-old half lounging on Betty Boop is growing

banyan roots, living ropes to stop his canopy from chasing
hothouse hot air balloons. The organic farmer, who wears
sheep-skin condoms, tries to convert the dandelions of his

waywardness, chanting *Oh Lamb of God* round and round with
LADOT tires. His understudy, barely appearing in the restless
window, corrupts the parsing. *Sins of the world have mercy*

on us. Or is it *Sins of the world, have mercy on us?* The three
Freshmen are played by extras who ripen before our eyes
from character actors to leading men and women. They fix

the rendezvous in their Gender Studies class: noon Tuesday at
the meeting of Kirkwood and rain, an event they easily
arrange, being the three graces. Not divine, yet his face is an

imprint of mine. Mine is a photographic negative of hers. Mike
noticed first. "You look more like your mom than you realize."
My mirror insists on the hard corner beneath her ear, the sag

above her chin, the shift from judgment to concern. My nose is as round as her thoughts, as low as her ambitions. The vagueness of one who neither hungers nor hunts rests in our

eyes. Go over the hill, slipping like a terrier in a tub, balls draped like a bulldog's jowls. You find a parking lot. Go round the same hill and confront a field that will not answer insults.

Agnus Dei on the bus after hours at a glory hole. You can't pinpoint when you fitted gods and sex with concrete taps and sent them to dance on a Vaudeville sea. How many birthdays

has she been my second skin? By what percentage has she raised my risk of melanoma? What benefit has she given besides briefly escaping into a new complexion? How many pounds of

dust has she added to the furniture? Does she notice the reminders my finger traces on the tabletop? Are we ever as mingled as the dead cells that alight there?

Salvage

Denny's Arbor Vitae

The Filling

1.
He turns the young Japanese maple upside down,
gently shakes, rights it, eases the rootball
into the newest hole,
cuts away burlap, like a paramedic
removing a hindering pant leg.

Blue rules the yard:
Russian sage smoking from long writhing grass;
Veronica cones; Bearded Tongues, their lips
sneering and puckering;
Blue Wonder's mounding pushy habit;
Bluebells suspended from their arches,
heads pointed down, afraid of passing out.

Obeying his blood's new dictate, he plants red.

2.
Slumped on the edge of the bed
in boxers, he glances blankly at
dream dirt on his hands and knows he's
been digging again.

There's an aerial view in his mind:
the cemetery, strange, unplanned,
graves not rectangular, not aligned,
scattered like buckshot or craters
where dogged meteorites struck.

Domed and Shoulder and Gothic tablets
are inscribed with dates he should recognize.
His wife's first breakdown, his
son's graduation, his granddaughter's
birth, his parents' jubilee.

3.
To read is to walk through someone's
personal cemetery. The graves are silences,
the corpses are cries.
Sometimes when I read,
a palm pushes the back of my neck,
prodding my medulla oblongata.
Satan doesn't tempt Christ.
He pushes him from the pinnacle —
a mass grave, gaping like God's will,
filled with one shove.

4.
It was a four-hour drive from
the top of Zone 5 to the bottom of 6,
past farms about to stir, along the skirts
of cities seemingly deserted, so hushed
he could've heard their yellow buzz if he'd stopped.

Now he walks past Catholic stones
herded in the shadow of Saint Mary's,
hemmed in by the horde of protestant granite.
He finds the trees overhanging
Martha Louise and Rollin Eugene.

Denny's Arbor Vitae

His flashlight shows white spots, places
where the stone is turning to marble —
no, just bird droppings. He wishes he
could wash them away.

Memorial Dawn in an hour.
Around ten, his brothers and their
wives, bearing silk flowers
and a miniature flag, will arrive and find
the vases inexplicably filled with
morning's deepest blue.

Timothy Robbins

Father and Son at Melody Mart

1.
The neck must be straight
like the yogi's back when he meditates.

Bridge and nut, chakras, align
to stop jangle and buzz.

To test, trap the E string between
nut and fret where neck and body unite.

The string must not touch the silver bars
just as the yogi must not touch the unkind.

Neither should the string be too high.
That is the sin of pride. Faults may be

rectified with the turn of an L wrench
just inside the sound hole

unless nut grooves are unforgiving
or friction has made them too lenient.

2.
I love the cooperation of my fingers
loosening and tightening the keys,
pulling the pegs like carrots from the ground,
massaging the fretboard with steel
wool and linseed oil,
lowering the ball-ends into the bridge,

Denny's Arbor Vitae

pushing the pegs in like the spikes of a tent,
threading the sharp metal ends of the strings
into the elusive holes
taking care not to bring pearls
of blood to the fingertips,
wrapping the strings around their metal poles
till their tautness makes them ring.

Listen to the beats. Trap
the low E between the
4th and 5th frets and strike.
Leave the A untrammeled
and strike again. Slow the
beats as the yogi slows his
heart, closer and closer till the
beats are one.

3.
His tools hung from pegboards mounted on the walls.
Families of screwdrivers large to small in panpipe arrangement.
Wrenches with creative jaw-tightening mechanisms.
Long-nosed pliers, wire cutters, spools of solder, soldering guns.
Stray drops of solder like frozen mercury tears.
Files to shape guitar and mandolin bridges.
Nails, screws, washers, bolts, gauges, calipers.
Wooden mallets reminded me of Geppetto and Saint
Joseph. Glue guns, staple guns, nail guns
(that always made me jump when they were fired) were the only
guns he hired. Petrified paintbrushes, wads of steel wool,
oil-matted dreadlocks lay like roadkill

next to handheld sanders and sandpaper worn smooth
as old breeches.
Planers overflowed with fragrant wood shavings like shorn locks.
Chunks of rosin glowed soft as amber.
A strobe tuner hummed with its glowing restless checkerboard.
Billows of antique player pianos showed the collapsed
lungs of small woodland
animals. Springs on the bottoms of snare drums mysteriously
rattled when an angry customer stomped by.
Bows' catgut hair (like Grandma's, like Zsa Zsa Gabor's)
had to be lovingly brushed and adored.
Guitars wore chokers on their necks and bridges.
Glue oozed like albino blood. Pianos stood with their inner harps
exposed, organs with their circuit boards pulled out.
Leslie speakers spun and spun and never got dizzier
than they wanted to be.

Denny's Arbor Vitae

Haines City

Herons step imperceptibly in failed
promises of rushing water.

Snowbirds come by choice and,
after exhaustive debates on which

routes to embrace and which to
shun, depart when warmth

turns to heat. Familiar names —
Tater and Toony, Pastor Atkins,

Pleakes Groceries, Stevens Feed
and Seed — are replaced by

names of new friends who shuffle
their days with long thin poles,

feast on clown-nose strawberries,
vie for the best roasting stick,

whisper who won't be back next
fall. On the south a flimsy fence

marks a field where cows, whose
presence I can't grasp, stir even less
than the herons.

Timothy Robbins

Breaking the Diaries

Her second husband hangs
with gulls and a Christ that lingers
after his cross decays.

She annulled him before
he could close that embrace
and we, the grandkids, knew
we were never to mention
his name.

She locked the license in
the trousseau she burned
with a tangle of storm-felled branches.

I wouldn't break her aluminum
Christmas tree or the seal
on her canning jars
or the promise I gave her
(it was tough as Swiss steak).

So why do I have no qualms
breaking these diaries?

I tell myself such simple keys
couldn't safeguard dark secrets.

Denny's Arbor Vitae

And diaries embossed with
beribboned kittens
couldn't harbor more than
a farmer's wife's undying
lookout for rain.

Around the dining room table we
peer at the ghostly graphite. Not
an inch of paper un-inscribed
(Great Depression habits)
with old fashioned cursive wobbling
more after each apoplexy, dwindling
as her body shrank.

I am a writer and yet I'm perplexed.
Why the loyalty to these annals?
Even in the last years when we stopped
replenishing them December 31st,
she took to filling 3x5 notebooks.

With the aid of a magnifying glass,
Dad reads word by word
as though epoxying shards
of a broken pot.

About my parents
(always called "the kids").
About the Methodist Sunday
school that loved to tease their
token Baptist. About children
she once baby-sat now sending
their own children to daycare.
About a phone call from freshman
me with the remark that my
boyfriend and I "sure were mixed up."

Dad lays down the loupe and
closes the book, saying without words,
"some words shouldn't be magnified."

I don't tell him to keep reading.
The real events aren't recorded here.

How she blotted out the name
of the Antichrist. How she
fed more people than Jesus —
hundreds of the mentally ill at
Muscatatuck, hundreds of 5th and
6th graders at Jerman Elementary.

How she led Mrs. Evans
back to her husband
every time she wandered
into our living room.

Weddings

then...
Western tuxedos were my brother's touch
along with his cowboy boots and a torch song
by George Strait. "Just be thankful men
can't wear hats in church," Mom pointed out.
Trying on my tux, I noticed the mirror bays
in Minear's Clothing were as I remembered —
though the multiplication of my image no
longer menaced. The Brannock device
still evoked torture, but now I knew better.
My brother wrestled Andrew, his soon-to-be
stepson, into his suit, jabbed in the shirttail, stabbed
in cufflinks and shirt studs, tightened the string
tie that reminded Andrew of Colonel Sanders,
pulled the laces of patent leather shoes (ceiling
light reflections, eyes of a black Kit Cat Clock).
In the vestibule we joked about what I should play
for the recessional. *Send in the Clowns?*
Comedy Tonight? I pinned my dad with a carnation
as though he were my prom date. Grandma,
wheeled in from the home, blurted over the vows.
A heckler of her own sanity, she decried, "the fatal
marshmallows nurses poison us with." The next
day, hung over, on bed's edge, I studied a photo
the family had never seen: me in a wide-sleeved
kimono with black and white striped hakama
standing much taller than usual in split-toe socks

and geta — a souvenir "for the kind American
who has befriended our son in a strange land."

now…
Drummers go before us.
Women bearing lit candles
walk with their backs
straight as the candles' flames.
The marhwa, Agni's fire, is kindled.
Around it we walk together.
Seven unwed friends paint
our faces, feet and hands with
sandalwood, turmeric, rose water.
We bathe in river and lake.
Your mother lays a garland
around my neck.
Mine does the same for you.
The bed is adorned with flowers.
Tobacco is offered.
Our families come with fruit,
clothes and gold in red boxes.
Half we keep, half return,
protection from greed and sign
we demand only as much as we need.
Broomsticks are burned.
Bamboo is sounded.

Laguna Beach

1.
The ocean pretends to foam at the mouth. I know
what it is to feign hydrophobia. The boardwalk
wobbles between sand and hotels. It's December 24th.
Pale-faced Hoosiers on Highway 1 look for a spot
to irradiate Christmas. "The city bought goats
to chew fire brakes." So Dad informs me.
Servants of Pan swallow treacherous kindling.
So I think. Hangover House scowls at Ocean on one
side, Canyon on the other. Built for an adventurer and
his ghostwriter lover (son of a Ghost Dance instructor).
Ayn Rand Olympians, they perished together
crossing in a junk from Hong Kong to this coast.

2.
Up to our shins in tide pool, picking up shells,
turning them over, putting them back like merchandise
we can't afford. Nearly naked kids romp in warm shallows.
Dad talks about his best friend's grandchildren.
Little League thrills, dance recital frills,
a six-year old girl whose seizures impose
family structure he envies. Later he attends candlelight
service. I linger in the room (the church being like a
lover you lavish credulity on till you catch him
in a lie). I watch the sun flirt with the balcony,
watch it back coyly into the Pacific.
Hoping to cruise, I look for the Rainbow Bookstore
Dad casually mentioned over lunch.

3.
This is the place — not the church, not the beach,
not Halliburton House — this is wonder's place.
The irony that I switched allegiance from the virgin
Christ to the lecher Pan and yet remain childless exerts
pressure as obsessive as the ocean's. Goats
carol and dance. Two gods lambada. The ghosts of
Halliburton and Mooney revive the Nanissáanah —
not on the moon-blanched beach, not in the black canyon,
not in their booze-reeking bedrooms.
Two explorers are lost at sea…

Denny's Arbor Vitae

Led by the Nose

In the shed I see light watchful as a shut-in.
I see gravel with a dog's brown spots.
Neither help. I place my feeble hope
in motor oil smell.

I know the tree swung a rope
much too long for a noose.
This knowledge is of no use.
Pungency of walnut hulls,
raccoon musk mixed with rotting leaves,
shake something loose!

The dog just back from the creek,
dripping like a sieve. Three-in-One
squirted between my flesh and
the blood-filled grip of ticks.
Gunpowder and Mom's panicky sweat
when my brother's curious paw
passed where there should have been glass.
Rusty plumbing. An old woman's gas.
Pine in the fireplace in front of which
we curled with a bitch and thirsty pups.
Whiffs of sulfur announcing
mentholated Pall Malls.

Timothy Robbins

Oil, why did my mother stop singing?
Musk and mulch, what forged me
single-minded as a key? Wet dog,
wet carpet, why did my relatives leave?
Why am I strong and unhappy?
Firing of a rifle, trickle of sweat,
scare up a ghost, wholesome or corrupt!

Denny's Arbor Vitae

Loner

"Just as I am," sung in Cantonese,
is drowned out by the talk of lunch-hour
all-you-can-eaters.
Hoosiers gorge themselves on
chow mein, mac and cheese, unlimited
refills of almost-jade-colored Mountain Dew.
A server, a Hong-Konger,
snatches back ravaged plates, her arm
surging exact as a snake.
The Lucky Buffet and her apartment
(one parking lot away from assisted living,
two lots from the nursing home)
are the places where Aunt Maggie
endures her final year.
Her bedroom shades are drawn
like her housecoat. Her TV
is populated by mutes.
"I've always been a loner," she boasts,
parting orange from peel.
We don't correct her, don't
remind her of all the babysitting,
4-H and debate team, a county of newlyweds
feeding each other her cakes,
extension club ladies painting covered
bridges by-number, rubbing soft tombstones
of high grassy graveyards,

the daughter and son she took in again
and again, their illegitimate children
that lit up the trailer, neighbors in Livonia
who taught her to golf and to idolize
Tiger Woods, wives from her husband's
banjo clubs, afternoons stifled by banjo drone,
a merciless army of overgrown bees,
the Mount Airy Baptist Sunday school class
waiting to welcome her back
after her thirty years of wandering
through Ohio, Michigan, Florida, Alabama
and Alaska. She coughs like
a dirty engine. She sweats like pot stickers.
She talks only about Bill,
how they went up in his bi-plane,
dumped sacks of flour, mischievous manna,
on a fellow prankster's roof.
How Bill rode the lawnmower to town,
not to be outdone by George Jones.
How Bill shot their son's goat
cause it chewed up her begonias.
How Bill cursed the tornado that mangled his plane,
making it look like "some God damned
modern sculpture."
Now she says she's a loner. And it's true.
She never speaks of meeting Bill up yonder.

Nest

Mine

That morning with my aunt at the strip mine,
I saw the exposed terrain as enticing skin,
my earth tones glowing as they would
when my eventual first lover undressed me.

I saw and heard the stillness as lifelessness —
as he would see my dawn-sleeping form
when he rose and withdrew, looking back just once.

I planted my folding easel in vulnerable sand,
saw the chemically colored puddles as the perfectly
natural pools of whatever SF novel absorbed me
that summer. I brushed on a broad underpainting
that would grow into a clean desolation.

Looking up from the canvas, I saw my aunt
striding her favorite golf course,
treading the Dead Sea with her Bible study group,
crossing a tropospheric Mojave in a biplane
with my uncle.

No hint of her future landscape stripped of him,
or her mind, barren and grand, stretching for miles.

Nannie

1.
Sink water adds exegesis to her
scripture-laden hands.
She keeps an eye on the games
outside and an ear on the bright
friend of her mornings, Dinah Shore,
sitting in a director's chair, high and
easy while Tony Orlando spars with
Ali then kisses lips would-be
champions dream of splitting.
She rinses and watches and says
nothing when bigger boys chase me
to the alley. Refuge is all she can
offer. A guilt she has no name for.

2.
A month after her first stroke she wrote me
a letter in lines like trembling capillaries.
Blood from her nose was water from a spring.
Gauze crowded into her nasal cavity.
"If I am here today it's only thanks to God's
powder." I got a good laugh, imagining that
powder, fairy dust colorful as the sprinkles
she used to scatter on our ice cream.
I wondered if it only worked on strokes
or if it was also effective against cancer, AIDS

or despair. I wondered if she thought blowing a
fistful in my face would clear up my sexuality.
Maybe, fearing straight would make me strong,
she would seal it in a canning jar tucked behind
the peaches on the pantry's highest shelf.

3.
...And in this corner, weighing in at
90 bounds, the Baptist Bomber. All the
wine she never drank has gone to her head.
All the plots of *General Hospital* are boiling in
her meticulously thinned blood. The nurses
are poisoning the Jello and the old woman
next to her is having an affair with my father.
It's raining in her room. Raining in the bed
that's not her bed at all. Soaking this food
she wouldn't feed a dog. It's pouring and it's
not her fault these half-witted nurses can't feel
their white uniforms sucking at their skin.
And her daughter, got-up like a middle-aged
know-it-all, has the gall to tell her the rain's
in her head. "You climb in this bed. I'll show
you a flood." Abruptly she boasts, "I walk all
over this town. Over to the Church. They got
a new river there where the young preacher
baptizes folks in white nightshirts. Last Sunday
the whole river was white! Nights I sneak over
to the Odd Fellows Home to peek at the old men

Denny's Arbor Vitae

though the window. Some of 'em see me and
try to catch me but I'm too fast for them.
That's how I got these skin tears: climbing over
barbed wire fences." The other day the
governor came and flew her in his copter —
so high, she didn't recognize her loved ones
or their sins.

To the Nursery with Dad

The two silences in the truck,
close but not touching,
goaded and guided by the
gear shift as we drive to the
nursery, want breaking.
We find the unmanned
office wide open. Invoices
lie trustingly on a metal
desk. One file drawer,
pulled out and bored,
waits while breeze and
coffee aroma swap
wordless gossip. A
monastic spell stops us
from calling out. We
roam the soft grounds
among potted, bagged
and labeled trees. The
pseudo monk, attending to
this or that vegetal need,
shimmers into view.
This enforced quiet
feels good, but not better
than the talk back in the
truck with a load of brown
bark in the bed. All
because I asked about
compost and mulch.

Western

Only my aunt in her coffin and her
absent daughter are vivid. Stephanie,
like Maleficent, uninvited, as though
that were punishment, as though any
force but her own windy curse could have
blown her through those heavy doors.
Her verve was as overpowering
as Linda Ronstadt's voice. Her sins
were covers, like the Sand Cutter's hits.
She rode with a cavalry of sinners,
straddling the turn of the decades
(that wild bronco) riding at a gallop,
leaving meek folk coughing in her
dust. I turn her into myth because I
barely remember: the tobacco
smell of soft plaid blouses knotted in her
cleavage; the turquoise clinging to her
finger when she played jump-bass
— Dylan's "Egyptian Ring," I thought.
She brought queer gifts: a pogo stick
(intuiting I'd enjoy bouncing on a pole)
and a lady's feathered cap because
I found it fancy. To France she sent
envelopes stuffed with Mary Oliver poems
and glimpses of her Boston marriage.
"City folk buy berries at the market while
their wild cousins shrivel in the parks."
I arrive at this ceremony, cantering side-saddle
where she would've thundered Western.

Wynwood Walls

Muralists redecorate the interior walls
with fake graffiti.
Ex-graffitists, lured by invitation,
tattoo the exteriors.
In a still storm of doubt and admiration,
I stand at attention, saluting my
memory of the clean and unclean
sides of the Berlin Wall.
Dad, Brother and I line up at a bar in a
city none of us knows,
far from fire, far from snow,
tasting designer beer on Christmas Eve.
"Tim wasn't in the creek that day."
Brother tells the childhood tale
of the snake he caught and tried to adopt.
For two weeks I'm outraged.
Then suddenly I'm thankful.
The tale of the snake I caught was tired.
The tale of my brother stealing the tale is fresh.
I feel my naked snake-thin torso
shiver in hesitant May warmth.
I feel brown water on legs
that for all an observers knows
are a cobra's tail. I see
the writhing sliver of daring in my fist
vanish like an image when the slide
projector is switched off.

Denny's Arbor Vitae

Raphael

Raphael, pushing CVS glasses on
his face, has forgotten the price
of Renaissance specs. He's working
on a Holy Family — as soft, as
dreamed as an early masterpiece.

I'm on a cushion. Mom's on the
ottoman. Between us, backgammon
spears aim at each other.
Dad reads and toe-strokes my
shoulder. The composition is

stabler than a dream, not as stable
as a painting. On the shelf, Grandpa's
firm throat is framed by his navy
collar. His cap is a dark halo.
His mouth is sensual and humiliating

like a uniform. His left hand rests on
the left leg of my father's baby overalls.
The buttons on Grandma's blouse
like cows in a field attract the child.
Sharing a mind, Mother and son

fix a point off to the right. Readers
are strewn throughout the flat —
some with the crossed arms of
Egyptian slaves in 1960s Panavision.
Some with arms extended in

welcoming rigor mortis. Did I
get these poses from bath-houses?
Hypocrite lecteur, when you read
readers did you think I meant you?
These holy trios, would they be truer

in the the desert's unflattering light
or in the cramped dim where the
Frankes held their breath? Something
or someone, not Herod's or Hitler's
horsemen, comes for us. No dream

in Dad's head urged us to flee
to these stanzas. We remind me of
Ling from China, Miguel from Peru,
their adopted boy from the Ukraine:
excited, unclear messages.

Denny's Arbor Vitae

Foundation

The old garage was a tetanus trap,
two stories high with barn doors on black
iron hinges. Dad tore it down and with
our unwilling help built what, 30 years later,
we still call the new garage.

My brother's in California
405-busy, excommunicado as Alcatraz.
I'm in Michigan tracking my lost self to
NA meetings. No one helps Dad restrain
the south wall of the cinderblock foundation,
pushing restlessly out like a pregnant gut.

I picture him kneeling on the blocks, all
his weight bearing down on the drill.

The bit and the man, too hot to touch,

He turns the I-bolts (which look like
Ankhs — the Egyptian glyph for Life)
into the holes. He drags a chain through their eyes
and with wrench and pipe pulls every muscle.

Trails

She had trouble taking her first steps.
One leg was shorter than the other.
The doctor put her in a cast — a hard little mummy below the waist.
It didn't stop her from pulling herself across the floor
to her father's knees. Her mom still remembers following
two lines of white plaster on the sidewalk
when she pulled herself to the neighbors two blocks away.
Once the cast was cut off no one could hold her back.
Seemed like overnight she was hitchhiking cross country
leaving a trail of Boone's Farm bottles, roaches,
abandoned debts, and wasted pardons.
The unevenness of her legs caught up with her somewhere in Alabama.
In her Facebook photo she's wearing orthotic shoes
and has gained so much weight her father wouldn't know her
if he was summoned to the morgue.

Narcissus Poeticus

Self-portrait with Udon

Night Visitors

1.
It's just after Christmas. I should be
wearing my new Christmas clothes.
Instead I lie naked under this hospital
gown, i.v. bags hanging down in place
of mistletoe, a seal of clotted blood
where my dick and the catheter kiss.
The fever that devoured my first night
has abated, leaving my mind prone to
hallucinations. But the nurses are not
witches. Their masks are just surgical
masks. The TV mounted in the corner
isn't spying, isn't trying to hypnotize me.
That's probably just footage from some
ordinary war. Not Goya's paintings
come to life — silent rifles silencing a
parade of Spanish peasants — Saturn's
mouth smeared with the blood of his
own child. The Titan naked. The child
naked. I have no recollection of being
stripped, a fate every human suffers at
the beginning and in the end. To bring
the nurses running when my bowels let
go I slip this clamp from my finger.

2.
In the middle of the third night, an encore
broadcast of *Amahl and the Night Visitors*
gets mixed up with my dreams, my delirium
and night visitors of my own. Two fat nurses,
more like thieves in the night than star-led
magicians, joke and gripe above my prone
body, my arms extended to receive stigmata
that never appear. They insert a snake into
my arm. It slithers up my shoulder. It will
spit venom into my vein every three hours
for a fortnight.

The boy in the opera up in the corner of the
room is a beggar like me, a musician and a liar.
The TV is a large bright star that sings. How
did I come here? Was it not my own lies and
the lies of night visitors seeking salvation in
my flesh that brought me to this bed? The
shepherd boy has his crutch and I have mine.
Together we sing our crutches into cures.

Denny's Arbor Vitae

Failure of a Miraculous Birthday

He turned twenty-one thirty minutes
before the end of his shift —
seven hours of a riveting machine
insanely chanting *Senator Trotsky,
Senator Trotsky*…

Afraid of the queer-baiting
taverns, he repaired to the 24-hour
Waffle House for silver dollar
pancakes that dared not mock his
size. He talked a little more
than usual with a cross between
Johnny Cash and Van Gogh's
wheat field with crows.

He enjoyed his surprise without
questioning it, hoping for a mind
that would always be two-stepping
with an immaterial partner,
riding a bucking machine,
being thrown, moaning
on a mattress the management
plopped down to avoid liability.

Bowing

When I was 14 I memorized Invictus.
All I remember now is, "My head is bloody but unbowed."
I think of all the bowing I've done since then.
Escaping eyes of bigger boys
who seemed offended by my existence.
Aping the obeisance of adults when
a man in a pleated dress intoned, "Let us pray."
Baring my nape to barbers' clippers.
Drinking from mountain brooks.
Standing solemn as a medalist
when a Saudi woman, careful not to touch me,
hung a charm around my neck.
Lowering my face into men's laps.
Getting down on my knees and searching the carpet for a
stray baggie. Praying, actually praying I'd never do that again.

Chuang Tzu's Butterfly

1.
I never wanted to get fucked till I met Brent.
After flickering black and white, nervously sharing
an armrest at the Marx Brothers' Festival,
watching the amazing Captain Spalding
who once shot an elephant in his pajamas,
I staggered home and found my prostate
for the first time, felt the bliss of blinding myself
with him, and as my self-possession trickled down
my ribs, became once and for all his prop,
his Panama hat, the flank at the end of his riding
crop.

2.
The fantasies began later, springing up like
forsythia in the cold of March. In one, we
are the Virgin Kings of the Harvest, coupling
in the high-timbered hut, our adolescence
culminating in the crush of the great logged
roof. In another, you bring a knife to bed
to leave no witness, not even one, that you
loved a man. In the most elaborate, you rig
a spike above the bed, that will strike through
your back, between your shoulder blades,
through your sternum, through my sternum,
pinning you to me, and me to our wedding pyre.

3.
Then I would sleep and dream of Harpo — the fish
in his pocket, a horn for a voice, silverware raining
from his sleeves. It seemed nothing stood between
him and the starlets' beauty. Till down an elevator shaft,
he found a harp that abruptly stopped the pain
and even its thought. And I would dream of you.
Maybe we would kiss. Or just your hand would fall
on mine, uncertain as Chuang Tzu's butterfly.

The Cut

I cut the side of my left thumb,
a scissor slip as I was patching the sofa.
Elizabeth Schwarzkopf in shaky black and white
sang, "Drink to me only with thine eyes."
Mike was tête- à-tête with an astrologer online
(prophecy steadieth his fears as music doth mine).

The thumb bled a little then stopped as though
it thought the effort wasted. If I were in a bleeding
contest, this would be humiliation. If I were a
Romanov, it would be a miracle. The likelihood
of this pinkish smear being virus-free
is a testament to human ingenuity.

Diagnosed

1.
How many people come to the woods,
after they're diagnosed,

to enjoy new trees, taut as
threads in the forest's warp?

I wrap my hand around their trunks,
hold them

as though they were staves, give them
a gentle tug. It's easy to shake their

ragtime leaves, to make them shimmy.
I remember my dad turning dreamy over

my mother's waist on their wedding day.

2.
I can imagine other humans here
more easily than I imagine a cure.

Survivalists drinking beer and
spitting into the fire words like

"liberal" and "homosexual agenda."
A unabomber writing his manifesto

Denny's Arbor Vitae

as fast as Kerouac — or rather typing it,
to echo Capote. If it were a much,

much bigger forest, I could picture
a diagnosee for every tree. In one vision

they stand straight and solemn
like druids ministering to tree spirits.

In another, they hang like Absalom in
a deadly tangle of leaves and hair; like one

of those broken branches snared in a leafy
net of twigs, unable to complete its fall.

3.
The healthy forest is studded with sick trees.
Coming here is like visiting a hospital or

a nursing home. Except many of the invalids
rise solid and strong and may stand so for

years to come, cordially hosting their parasites,
stoically regaling their infections.

Timothy Robbins

Fault Lines

My fault the swollen uvula, the
rusty nails posing as relics, the
ethical impasse with Venetian
Carnaval masks, the obscene love
letters fed to mail slots; not locking
the door the night all the stars
pointed to burglary, choosing
to get laid rather than help a friend,
my parents' aging Christmas-less
knees, sunsets like busted
taillights, nights gooey as oil spills,
romantic frauds, the frog-eyed kid
who left unsatisfied, not giving
encouragement to a talentless
busker, the volcanic pimple on my
ass that scared off the handsome
spanker, losing my brand new
hushpuppies, spiking the Korean
guy's beer, not eating the pork chop
laboriously prepared for me, not
staying awake all night on the
corrugated roof, not striving for
organic unity, not insisting on organic
produce, having a Godzilla-sized
carbon footprint, leaving a pallid
molted rubber on the storeroom floor,
making my sixth-grade buddy think
our friendship was a psych experiment,
pushing sad men's hands from my thighs.

Abandoned Thoughts

I rubbed prayer all over my body,
glistening by day like a sunbather,

glowing by night with the Barnabas
Collins model standing in for my

nine-year-old nightlight,
phosphorescence too gentle to

peel. I spiced my eyes with
psalms. They burned like pepper

spray, branding my corneas, cattle
with neither rancher nor rustler.

My soul strained its muscles and
reached only itself, a touch suddenly

devoid of intent.

Advice

Glory when you realize a man who wants to harm
you is about to sell you a precious secret. Come
back again and again to the man who bred you,
his glistening scalp, a melon so exotic you won't
know how to ask the grocer for it. Discover how its
own tangy juice smears its uncracked rind. He's
just been born again. The nurse has not yet washed
the blood away. Let Japanese and bearded iris teach
you when to shiver. Let children wiggling out of
water, stamping on hard wet sand, give you tips as
restless as beads of water. A light hangs on a chain
from the pergola. Its sway hesitates between back
and fourth and round and round. Be like the patio,
not clear yet if you're thinking about a man or a
woman. Let your earrings emulate your shy neighbor's
hanging plants. Read books with words dark as
rained-on grass, tree trunks, blacktop, clothes
sucking up to skin. Each word slides like mascara.
The water on my cheek, pressing down my hair, hanging
like spiders from my eyelashes — these are all part
of the book, the part that makes it worth reading.
Let these be the last lines you write — not a suicide
note, but as final as one. Beware the greed good poetry
breeds, greed for more and more verse. Soon you
won't get through the day without a shot.

Denny's Arbor Vitae

Assets

I knew you'd be chatty and
curious when we were through,
when the air that had been
eyeing us with feelings we
couldn't guess regained its
fish-eyed stare. Knew
you wouldn't resist my curiosity.
Proud, not obnoxiously so, you
showed me your collection of
rare money lined up in leatherette
albums — bills sleeping like
the Declaration of Independence,
coins like moons gazing through
portals. I wondered: will I
some day be part of your past
preserved in an acid-free mat?

Astrology

You call yourselves constellations?
You're not even stars —
not ones I would piss on.
You're already wet. A sky full
of soggy matches while the denizens
of this little world shiver around
piles of twigs, fumbling
to light each other's exploding cigars.
We have heard of comparable
twig piles with more fiery
temperaments. My God will never
bush-burn. Like me, he's
terrified of fire. His commandments,
or horoscopes, sound like this: Strive
not to emasculate your doubts, but
to purify them. Be wary but not
scornful of those who convince
themselves their showers are
bruising them. Resemble Paul Klee,
who found Wagner's and
Debussy's operas beautiful.
Pieces you've started that haven't
taken form are blessed with
possibilities and problems
that swirl together like
flushes, the baptisms bullies

Denny's Arbor Vitae

bent you to, unwittingly teaching
the truth about genuflection.
Give unstintingly to the sense
there is light you itch to unleash,
light you must unlock if you wish
(and you do) to see my face.
When you realize
you cannot make such light, be
an artist who makes masterpieces.
Hear electric discharge
and remember your shirt going up,
catching on the ends of your arms
raised like a referee's affirming
a touchdown or a marshaller's guiding
a taxiing jet with a gesture.

At Twelve

At twelve I heard Christ
cry, "Fry me!"
Bigger boys were playing
Burn Ball but didn't
get the allusion.
"Forgive my lack
of sin," he called again
with his voice like a
teacher's bell or maybe
a paddle. I looked out
the window at the
basketball courts.
"I am deaf! I am lame!
Heal me that I might hear
the shouts and run and shine
in the game." I stopped
my ears with spitballs.
He sighed and
switched to blackmail.
 "If you won't release
me, others will."
And I watched him walk
straight to the boys that
were all insolence, strength
grace, poise.

Atripla

At check-in I asked the clerk
to leave a pill in place of
the pillow-mint. We have
such choices. On the way
up, I flipped the keycard
palm to palm. The magnetic
strip reminded me of a
matchbox striker. I thought
of the sparkling keys of former
times and reminded myself
how quickly they tarnished.
Most of the time his eyes
showed that dullness. They
glinted only when he was
deceiving. Only when the
thoughts bending his path
were pedestrians he knew
he could hit and run or hit and
Samaritan. The last time I
opened a hotel room with a
brass key, I was turning down
a hooker because I'm gay.
Now I wish I'd motioned her in.
No doubt she needed the pay,
as I needed a mom to hear my
prayers, to touch my forehead,
to ask if I wanted the door ajar.

Robber

Ballet

The ease with which he and I assume
our positions is dizzying. It's all decided
in a glance. No interrogation. No negotiation.
Each knows instantly he's what the other
is looking for. Every entrechat is executed
with the grace and force Nijinsky used on
Ukrainian soldiers camped outside Vienna
after the War. Russian accents and balalaikas
drew him like poison from a wound, lured
him from madness and diary silence. He
leapt with sparks from their fire, came down
on point and stepped into their thoughts. One
brooded on April. One fought the feelings
of besieger for besieged, urges as convoluted
as fertile soil. One recalled how he loved the
quarters where Panzers, near-sighted monsters,
lumbered. Whereas quarters that lay down
without a fight bored him. One relished
identical feelings for bodies he raped. One
listened for youth's stones splashing like
bridges the Red Army cast into the Danube.
One wept for the polio-stricken sister
he used to dance for.

Sal Mineo

The doors are unlocked. Your parents
lie in soundproof slumber.
We crawl across the roof,
like the Cat in "To Catch a Thief,"
(so we think), and lower our-
selves down a trellis
that has barely begun to put out roses.
For an hour we dodge harmless
headlights, convinced Moonie
vans are trawling for young recruits.
Back in your room, sunk in beanbag
chairs, we pore over Penthouses
swiped from my brother. I wait in vain
for you to find the letter where a
straight reader confesses
"I really dug what that guy did to my dick."
In the kitchen you eat leftover
octopus. I smear jam on Wonder Bread.
A headline spread on the counter says an actor
we never heard of is dead, felled by
one perfect stab.

Denny's Arbor Vitae

Christ

His not being real
does not interfere
with my loving him.

I will dismember him,
as I must, but not
like a wild beast

driven by hunger
and bloodlust. I will
imitate as best I can

a watchmaker
dividing the charming,
tiny, intricate works

of an exquisite pocket
watch, taking care
that nothing should

get lost or bent, that
the thing might be
put together again,

passed down to my
son with a manual
that instructs: This is

a timepiece. This
is how it's made,
unmade, remade.

Cotton Candy

Cornrows

A woman cornrows sleepy curls,
steadying her child between
cushiony thighs, neutralizing
the train's jostle — a little.
She lifts a slice from brow to nape,
braids it front to back,
ties it at the scalp,
moves to the next row
glancing down as seldom as
I glance at the notebook in my lap.
The woman scans new riders
as though they were bar codes.
The girl resists
no more than a corpse resists
a mortician. I turn to the window
and see a reflection —
Rimbaud's nuns pinching
lice from a new poet's locks.
Barely aloud he admires,
"If the mother is Madame Defarge,
what dooms she knot in her
sleepy child's hair!"

Timothy Robbins

The Ghost of the Rose

Collaborators that never meet.
That need interpreters.
That are tossed with the
programs.

A few shine to this day.
Diaghilev, Nijinsky, Weber.

One, in a rush, falls through
a trapdoor. His rings leap
and run not very far, then
relax unharmed on a
concrete floor. I cast myself

as the debutante in soaked
gown, folds acrid from
waltzing, arches aching,
stomach growling —

too late to wake my maid.
In the lobby, whiskey
sour in hand, bored by
well prepared accolades,

all I feel is the closeness
of my coat and the dark
that will walk with me
arm in arm, gossiping

Denny's Arbor Vitae

about the costume rushed
in on the last train, silk
petals torn and askew, the
set-painter kneeling in place
of the costumier, Vaslav

wincing and cursing in
Russian as pins through
the tricot prick his skin;

cursing the man in evening
dress and top hat, whose
voice was too self-assured
at the Europa Hotel; who

made Vaslav "tremble like
a leaf" when they made love
moments after they met.

"Tell me again about the
stage hands who night after
night catch him in warm
white towels. Tell me

about the servant gathering
petals from the boards
and the costume mistress
backstage
when the stars go drinking
and screwing."

"With curling iron
she reshapes wilted silk."

Gita Raga Rag

Reading the *Gita* at sixteen sowed me with visions of voluptuous
Gods coupling on Methodist pews.
By seventeen, free from bonds of attachment, I stood tiptoe on the
steeple and asked Morning an impertinent teenager's questions.
Morning, are you like Jazz, like porn —
undefinable but known?
Matutinal transcendence of civilization is clear each time your
colors churn. You are a priori fresh,
a quality I forgot around my 40th spring. At fifty I'm free from
night sweats, from changing pjs five times before dawn, from
neurosyphilis technicolor dreams,
from fretting who my next fix will come from, from pinpricks that
peppered me like voodoo Barbie
and the belief that bruises are passports to asylum, from privacy
invasions, well and ill meaning, from
spirit-killing thoughts pretending to be trick-or-treaters
playing tunes on the doorbell of my will to live,
from boredom and the urge to enshrine it, from regular cars
straining to be bumper cars and vice versa, from prayer gusts that
force one to gasp, from coffins deep in deep-freeze delusions, from
salesmen scribbling graven images on receipt books,
from vitamin-deficiency avatars. From storm. From heatwave.
From the grid's fragility, susceptible as our brains.
Later I'll notice WE Energy's apology in my voicemail, uniting
thousands. It's 4:00 a.m..
LED-jungle-eyes blink, blink, and close, our machines deciding

we're not worth devouring. The only
glow in the complex is from the Indian mother smoking on her
balcony, burning, inhaling,
releasing her matins to Agni. On the couch, under quilts, it's like
we're sharing a sleeping bag, camping out for ninety minutes
without a campfire. It reminds me
how much I wish I'd known you as a boy when insects hypnotized
you and you hypnotized them.
When Hanoi blackouts were scheduled,
routine as school and denunciations.
We talk about your birth. Your reluctance to emerge and how your
grandmother walked your mother back and forth, hoping to shake
you loose. You came out blue as Krishna in a hospital I picture as
a mosquito-netted hut. At fifty-one, to remind myself I'm still
bound, I bid for Liberty Bond posters online.
My favorite shows a dark figure in an orange and yellow sky and
bay, one arm raised to catch the ankles of a Fokker Eindecker
or a Sopwith Camel.

Lay of the Land

1.
Monday there was a new sound
in the morning chorus: water splashing
into massive wine goblets.
Another sound on Tuesday: the toneless
friction of an apprentice finger
riding a massive brim.
Wednesday the friction began to
squeak and moan, the braking of a train
pulling into an empty depot.
Thursday, glass sang — the devil's true violin.

2.
Sparrows come for breakfast,
doves, for brunch.
The air outside and in
was looser yesterday.
The reason is a secret I will
tell you when I trust you.
I will whisper it with my scent.

I do not covet your wife or
your ass.
Your house is another story.

The penthouse grabbing day's first light —
a trailer with its rummage-sale yard,
its whirligigs and dogs —
the RV that flits like a butterfly

Denny's Arbor Vitae

from park to park — the sparrow's
downy body — the pigeon's
orange eye — I see and I must inhabit.

3.
Habitat envy I inherited from my mom.
Envy of the loquacious from my dad.
My envy of the ground springs from my
male barrenness. I envy my discontent's
elusiveness. It escapes me every time.
I envy Baudelaire his face that matches
his poems so well. He was a walking
advertisement for his sickly FTD.
I envy trees that cast dappled shade. My
shadow is so solid, so un-quivering. My
envy of men with smooth legs was inspired
by a tennis player at my high school and
reinforced by a man I saw in the laundromat
with vinyl thighs and a pouch for a crotch.
He looked out the window and clapped his
knees like a wind-up monkey's cymbals.

4.
A desert city. The temples, the mansions,
the hovels, the baths, the armory, the confident
wall, the markets, the prison — these together
were my many-headed god. Buying, selling
thieving, arresting, praying, fucking, giving
birth to life and death, these were my sins,
for in this wicked city every thought was stained.

The sinning moved on. The ruins remain.

5.
Now that I've settled into the
stillness of reading, they're back: the
pigeon with his stabbing head, the sparrows
so light they can't stay down. They're back
but they don't come close.
I am not as gentle as Francis.
I wouldn't preach to them if I could.
Less gullible than their grandsires,
they wouldn't listen if I did.

6.
I avert my eyes from a woman sunbathing
in view of a hundred windows.
Even on this safe and gorgeous day
it makes me think of Kitty Genovese.
Maybe I would overcome my modesty
if I thought my skin would darken with poems.
A husky fertilizes the ground.
His eyes blaze yellow. Dandelions bloom
clear, blue, sexy. I'm trying to fly off
but I'm not the leaf a weakling twig holds;
I'm a flag whose pole is a domineering matriarch.

7.
The air is liberating
like mentholated sinus spray.
I peel skin gloves from my hands
and find another pair beneath.
I think, "This is the last one.
If I just get it off, my hands will be free."

Denny's Arbor Vitae

Mercy

I want you to be as merciful as you claim to be.
Whether you exist or not, whether or not you're
coming back, I want you to be so merciful
you ache.

For I am the legion and the pigs and the cliff
over which they hurl themselves, and the
farmer who loses his stock, and the farmer's
wife calling him a clumsy son of a bitch,
and their children going without supper,
and his debtors who don't get paid and all
the things in his house that are repossessed.
I am everyone in this story except you and
the man who was de-possessed.

I want you to be merciful even though mercy is
foolish and contrary to natural law, even if
seven times seventy was boastful hyperbole.

For I am the son who loves his mother and
father but dishonors them behind their backs.
I am the parent who gags his noisy child
when I'm trying to read. I am the one who
does the least and then worries he hasn't
done enough. The one who seeks pleasure
without consequence. The poet who spends
hours adjusting texts few will read. The tree
that bears poison figs and the tree that happens
to be fig-less when you happen along on your
donkey, feeling peckish and omnipotent.

One Gate into the City

In a hotel room smaller than we expected
I think of the many expectations we've devoured,
some bigger, some smaller, some just
what our appetites required. Because of its size it's
a treehouse. Because of its price and its courage
(despite acrophobia) — and most of all
because of my my excitement it's the penthouse
of treehouses. Despite its size, it's a forest
that stretches as far as the eye can see
if the eye is a buzz saw. Intermittently in its green
expanse some light flickers — maybe a fire, maybe
a flare tossed up by a desperate hiker, maybe
a bewildered police car's flashing tic.
The towny poet has returned to the city.
The taxis he sees darting lane to lane
like dreams under skin bridges
turn mad corners from sheer delight —
dogs' elation at the appearance
of a human, master or stranger.
The small town poet is both. See how the stately
buildings stand like domestics on a manor estate,
the butler with his Miltonian diction,
the housekeeper with her dull efficiency,
the valet with his asexual circumspection.
The poet is returning for the millionth
time to the millionth city in the millionth century.
The great welcome surprises him
as it did the first time and every time since.

Denny's Arbor Vitae

Suddenly he's aware of all those cities in his head.
And with them Augustine's,
Plato's, Moore's — all seduced by urban sprawl.
The dizzyingly light weight makes him giggle,
and on that giggle he rides,
as if it were Christ's donkey.
All he needs is a little spending money
and to get out before the desk clerk and the mayor
realize that they reared this for him,
that the first night rain, a wet ticker-tape parade, is for him.

Potential

Volume 10. The Golden Book
Encyclopedia. "The boy was not well
liked. The story of his life is one of
many quarrels with popes."
Adam and David —
blue and white cartoons,
their groins smooth and
white as the bowl I ate Corn
Flakes from. I trembled in the tub,
worried what would happen to me
when I was grown. If he had
already faced the giant, the boy
would clutch in one fist
the dripping head by its hair and
in the other a sword (a weapon
no shepherd could afford)
tempered by Philistine blood.
His right hand has taken the sling
I'm tempted to see as a loin-
cloth, his only clothing just
pulled off or about to be donned,
resting in the crux of his raised
shoulder and turning neck.
His left hand at his thigh is strong
not from fight but from herding
earth's gentlest creatures.
The fingers, curling as though to
scratch, cradle the agent of the
tall man's fall. The body which

furs and maidens will warm in
old age is sovereign. He feels the
tremor against his soles, still
distant. Time to imagine his curls
caught in a crown.
For those of us who will
never be king, whose forms are
never complete there is no more
perfect expression of the
potential than this unfinished
slave writhing in his sheet,
this promise of an unfinished
grave. I have seen you
stretched on my bed in this
very pose, one hand behind your
head, fingers knotted
in your disheveled hair, the other
hand lifting your shirt, leaving
your stomach bare. Your fingers
explore the depression at the
lower tip of your
sternum. Your equally
unfinished mate strains at his
bonds, flexing for fight.
You and I defeat them all. No
scribbler, no sculptor, no tribal
god will make stones breathe,
let alone excite them.

Residuals

1.
Our quarrels forget us, run off to a bigger city.
We hope they'll come back for holidays. Liven up the place.

Our sexual impulses turn into tabbies. They don't want
to be held. We don't want to get clawed.

We suffer them to slide from our laps.

2.
Your bones are getting sharp. I fear their cut.
Your hips are narrower than my laptop.
My fingers on the tiny keys, typo
hilarious, perilously circumspect pleas.

I think about this as you stagger home looking
like Jackie Cooper
returning from the Children's Crusade.

3.
I don't find a fitting coffee table. Outside the Salvation
Army Store a conniving old woman calls me an angel
and kisses my left cheek (I don't turn the right)
because I give her ten bucks, knowing you'll reward me
when I tell you.

This, I never told. We were renting
Tama and Laura's basement. They needed cash,
we needed digs, and though it was annoying

we put up with the clicking of their Alsatians'
claws on their floor/our ceiling. Maybe we
should have tried to understand those canine
messages. But neither of us could be bothered
to learn Morse Code. It was the day
Tama re-welded the penis on an outdoor Adam,
vandalized by we never knew who — a puritan,
a feminist, a drunken frat boy? You were at work.
I saw your brother coming three blocks away,
seeking your company, which he'd never done before —
your counsel, if he could get up the nerve —
finding only me, as stuck-up as ever — and even
more alarmed by his allure.

4.
I who truly love silence,
why do I seldom seek it?
When my man says nothing
why don't I feel it as strength?
Why do I swap
Humphrey Bogart for
Woody Allen?
Why do I ignite my man
like a firecracker?
If I act like this, I who love silence,
what can I expect from silence-haters?

5.
I tell you I love coarse dry breads.
That's not the whole truth. I also love white bread
my saliva turns to mush.
I love "wheat" bread that's really just
unbleached Wonder. I love flat breads.

They make me feel biblical.
I loved the swampy Essene bread
I used to buy from the Orthodox monastery
in Indianapolis. That was when I lived on Alabama
Street, walking-distance from a club where I could pick up
a new man every night. I loved penetrating,
albeit barely, the monastery's hushed obscurity.

6.
All the men I've slept with are out there somewhere.
The sun comes to life in a root beer bottle empty
as last night's man, his tan as darkly translucent as
the neck from which he drank. His sleeping face
senses how hard the music is trying to be insincere.
The foot sticking out from the afghan would
make a baby leer.

7.
Sometimes I listen with my eyes closed.
Sometimes, with them open.
Jesus suggests there are times I should
pull them out. Another voice enjoins me
to rip off my ears so I can't hear
his mad suggestions.

8.
I want to write a poem about
Billy Strayhorn. What a name! One of the
few people musical enough to break Duke
Ellington's heart.

I'm setting up a poetry factory in my room.
Soon I will call in the Luddites.

Denny's Arbor Vitae

Tight Places

I buy St. Vincent Millay's *Complete Works*
for two and a half bucks. The women she loved,
the orgasms they gathered (and endlessly discussed)
are worth more to me than all her verse. I wonder
if her approach to one discipline was as meticulous as it was to the other.
"When you were a boy, you would look out the car window
like you could see across the fields something I couldn't."
The saddest thing my mother ever said to me.
It made me happy. Should I be more careful with my words?
Should I be less careful?
I look at a stain on the ceiling, about three inches across,
and think of the miracle of thousands of bats
pouring like dark wedding wine through a fist-sized cave entrance.
Who will listen with me to Mahalia Jackson singing,
"You saw me crying in the chapel?"
You, Hussein? You, Abdulrhman? You, Shareef?
Three names on a roster of fourteen.
Will you gather me like warm linens in your arms?
Will you and your cousins iron me as Mary Sue's friends
ironed the one hundred table cloths she bought for her daughter's
wedding, knowing she has seven more daughters to go?
Will you convince me that despair is liberating?
I swear the sun went down four times today,
went down like a boxer, and struggled back up all but once,
amid a din in which cheers and boos inextricably tangled.
Yes, I am lying, and like all liars
I am only interested in what is clear and what isn't.
When Mahalia Jackson sings slowly,

she makes even Joyce Kilmer's Tree sound majestic.
Will you understand if I say that I sing gradually?
Pizza on my shirt. Motherly bedspread on the bed
(white chenille looks as tasteless as cottage cheese).
Brown bruise on the ceiling. Record on the stereo.
Ungenerous thoughts on my conscience.
The last season feasts on the sky. I can hear its digestion.
No need to spare the appetite; it won't be used again.
I'll work on this poem tomorrow:
Highway 46 instead of I94 because Dad's too old to hurry.
I try to remember which road into the woods
(inconspicuous as the bats' front door) leads to John's cabin,
which I walked to one night, two hours on unlit road.
Will it be safe to tell Dad about my addiction when dementia
robs him of the capacity to worry? Will he think I'm
announcing the advent of a grandson?
For now, I'm most concerned with this list of names
followed by test scores, the lowest 83, the highest 97.
Six hours a day for six months with these people.
We reclined together in Adler Planetarium
on a day when snow far outnumbered stars.
We were bored at the Potawatomi Zoo in South Bend,
even more bored than the animals.
In the dark of the bus coming home from Six Flags
Narongchai's cheek roosted on my thigh.
Fourteen people. I remember three.
After twenty-five years all I can say is
students are as innumerable as Wonders of the World.

Common Law

Mike on the Sofa

Denny's Arbor Vitae

Passover

End-of-winter
bugs are drawn
to our front door's
extreme white.

You would never
kill them.
I'm not so careful
with my Karma.

Come. I want to
show you the blood
smeared on the wood
in the hope

that any passing
god, bearing curse
or bearing good,
will pass us by.

How You Came to Me

Geese claim the skies as skateboarding teens
claim the sidewalks; as drunken ex-privates
carol in the dark till their voices crack;
as tourists from the latest prosperity
shout in duty-free shops, cocky in their unintelligibility.
I choose this river-bend because here even geese
are circumspect. They come for shallows
and soft level ground on which to lay their eggs.
The shapes of their legs, their long supple
necks, (curving downward to graze,
twisting to pick mites from their backs)
preserve their evolutionary past.
From a hopeful distance, I watch
a committee of five — worried, officious or
curious? — approach. Two veer to my left,
two to my right. The middle one keeps on,
sizing me up at each lurch, coming close enough
to catch bread I toss in his path. Briefly,
unreasonably he trusts, then waddles back,
honking delight, disapproval, bellyache.

Denny's Arbor Vitae

Couvre-Feu

Not bedclothes — small,
even smaller than now,
we managed to cover
the mattress.

It was in a restored
Victorian inhabited by
vows and men who swore
them.

Sitting up like mothers
breakfasting on Mother's
Day, we watched a VHS
African Queen.

No more embarrassed
than the nearly nude
Christ on the wall,
we didn't pray, like Rosie,
to be judged by our love
and not by our fall.

Timothy Robbins

The leeches were kissers.
The sexual act, a blood-
letting. As the window lost
its fight with TV,
I wondered how we'd
cover the land.

A nurse dragging a sheet
over a newly dead face?
A landscaper laying burlap
on unrolled turf?

A maiden with her
hand on her muff?
A boy disguising
his spasm as a cough?

Denny's Arbor Vitae

The Prayer

As a puny teenager and well into my
buffed-up twenties,
I thought I was praying for cocks to
rise in me,
moons into the dark, suns into the day.
When an apostate rabbi at the
soup kitchen told me
we can't make petitions till they're
granted, I argued.
Ferocious, logical, arrogant, young.
He nodded a sigh and dropped a scoop
of wet spinach on a tray.

A few of the invasions of my sky:
The Fourth tricked my
eyes into thinking they were 12 again.
Japanese fire flowers
one at a time
insisted the heavens are
the darkest garden.
Dead Black birds
planted that garden in Arkansas.
The Challenger snowed on the
Atlantic. My French hosts looked at me
as though the shuttle was my lover.

Now I know my prayer was for
the starts of one man's days.

Some speechless as eclipses.
Some mooned and sunned with questions.
Do you need the car this morning?
Who put the flashlight in the freezer?
Are your fingers and toes still numb?

Bright Sleep

Marriage

To wake in the night rising in your mouth,
tapping your soft palate, passing all
the points of articulation like an intoxicating word.

To know that hunger for this, for me, broke your sleep.

To feel my extremities one by one
swim beyond my reach, beyond my call.

To watch my legs flail, flail, falter, fall still
like legs I saw in a movie once
of a man choked to death behind the Iron Curtain.

To feel power rush helplessly out of me
as dark clouds pass
revealing white clouds that pass
revealing blue sky that passes…

I guess marriage isn't like that. At least not ours.

Timber

His skin like quarter-sawn oak,
perfectly cut growth rings running

straight and tight the length of all
that is long or flat. I gaze on dark

swirls of medullary rays and discover
inner forms. Wavy interlocking grains,

evocative of entwined limbs,
meticulously buffed and brushed with

coat after coat of thinnest shellac.
My face shines in his dark glass. He holds

the finish, resists twisting and warping,
is impervious to degradation.

Denny's Arbor Vitae

You are Sitting at the Table

preamble
I keep thinking about the groom's side
and the bride's and how at the reception,
amid bad dancing to corny music,
in boozy informality (antidote to
ceremony) this segregation gets flushed.
The couple drives off to recuperate.
The newly connected families droop at
the first of many messy tables, beginning
the long interweaving of chronicles.

amble
North from the Cumberland Gap,
from the Ohio to the Big Blue River,
Chrysler attracts and a girl remembers
a school where spellings, hardy as wildflowers,
solid as big, lovely as blue, entered her world.
She remembers her father's lap.
The watch twirling, cajoling memories
of unforeseeable, punishing slaps.
Fleeing her village, your grandmother
is a fulcrum; the long pole
stretches before and behind her,
Older Sister in the pioneering basket
— Younger Sister, lagging, balancing.
Car-less, his wife in labor,
Dad sprints to the parsonage.

The parson fills the doorway,
impatient as a comic to relay a new joke.
With Deborah's wisdom a kitchen voice bellows,
"Arnold, get them kids to the hospital!"
Enfants terribles. Two Vietnamese children
run naked in the street.
I never see the girl. I never see the boy.
She's a photo in a thousand papers,
on a thousand websites,
flapping featherless wings, rushing toward us with
the black cloud, the clothed, the uniformed.
He's a figment I conjure
from childhood tales you tell me
of a street purged by the morning's
dose of monsoon and unwary passersby
harmlessly doused from a hose
wielded under cover of your family's outdoor shower.
Eight thousand miles away
My brother and I wiggle through
a sprinkler's cold falling arches.
Barefoot, we dodge clover bees.
At the bathroom tap we feel balloons grow
heavy like bloated bellies.
Not to cleanse your feet, but to make them
deportable, your father leads you to the mosque.
It will take more than this to induce the Party
to brush your dust from its feet.
Seven years old in a camp in Thailand
you hold it in for weeks on end,
terrified of falling into foreign toilets.

Denny's Arbor Vitae

You're constipated to this day.
In the attic of your aunt's house in New Orleans
you and your sisters warm
your hands on sewing machines,
piecework far past midnight.
When staying up late is still
thrillingly forbidden, Dad comes
to the foot of the stairs and calls up softly,
"Grandma, are the boys in bed?"
"Shush, you'll wake them,"
as we squeeze in tighter, one
on each side of her in that wide
green chair, eyelids struggling
with TV's relentless, beckoning flicker.

post amble
A poet and a mathematician
set up house midway across the Bridge of Birds.
You bring your numbers. I bring my words.
We both bring scraps of tales
to burn in a barrel at our forebears' feet.

Another Flag

I flap above an unknown
soldier who keeps sitting up,
blurting out his name,
having to be shushed
like a kid bored or over-
excited at a funeral.

I'm relieved when the wind
lets me drop.
I don't really want to ride it.
I want a custodian to
unhook and spread me out,

my pinkish white overlapping
your brownish yellow,
a flag across a box too wide
to be buried
in a standard plot.

Denny's Arbor Vitae

At Home

Six months make
an indelible depression
in the cushion where
he sits and sleeps,
his laptop on a
tray-table pinning him in.

At the end of one
complaint, he finds
another.

He talks the way he
eats cashews,
regaling himself down
to the last tip.

I wake in an
overheated room and
blame the heat for
the dream of the
Beau Monsieur
with too much mercy.

I assume the face
behind the visor
is his or mine,
ambivalence that
frightens rest.

How to Break the News to the Nguyens

Lure your family to the dim
-sum shop on Geary. The one
like the inside of a train or
a church aisle without the rest
of the church. Woo them with
 good or sad news. Tell them
you've updated the date of
your birthday. Tell them
you're commemorating an
obscure milestone in Ho Chi
Minh's journey. Squirm at no lie.
Get them to the table. Have the
waitress wheel me out on a
cart: irresistible, divvied up,
bite-sized on a score of white
plates, later to be twirled on
long sticks.

Denny's Arbor Vitae

Bird

I used to bitch
at you for leaving
the lights on.

Now I brighten
hall and kitchen
before you wake.

The bird I make
hides in all birds'
nests.

The bird you birth
rides its threat
as no crow ever

rode black cry,
no hawk ever dove
from screech.

Tomorrow I
swallow my 52nd
year like a plate

of eggs. The songs
my bird sings
add.

The anthems your
bird announces
equal.

Dressed Up

The first day of the semester
he disguises himself as a metrosexual.

The bathroom mirror,
a merciless critic, ignores the clock
thundering in his chest, the comb
shaking in his hand.

Tomorrow his students will be
shocked and relieved
when he saunters to the lectern
in baseball cap and jeans.

The first few years I dreaded
first classes. Now I relish
the chance to be the calm one —

Judy Garland's mother backstage.
The chauffeur keeping the engine
running. Jeeves, whose inscrutable
judgments go unchallenged.

Denny's Arbor Vitae

I linger with my arms crossed
atop the steering wheel,
watching him march into the lecture
hall, remembering how spruced up
he was the first Thanksgiving
with my family,

as ironed and creased
inside as out, the interloper,
the Vietnamese boyfriend
wanting to look as out of
place as he felt.

The Treader

You're the opposite of the lame
man in the Gospels. You walk
and walk, going ghostly through
walls I put up to prove they can't
stop you. You're a somnambulist
who knows exactly where he's going
and why the only way to get there
is on foot. Your walking feels so
good you get hooked and soon
you're walking over those you meet
including me, including yourself.
Luckily you don't need a miracle
vendor to stop you. Any Joe who
tells you, "Put down your bed and
sleep," will do.

Fuller Street Daruma

Endowment night, two Baptists
at the door. "Two? Are you sure?"
Yes, I am. I refused them
the night before. "Did you plead,
'Shake the dust from your feet?'"
I gave them a courteous
just a minute then proved how well
I ignore.

His index and middle finger
pressed in a Scout salute, he taps
his temple and stutters, "t-t-t-truth
is out there!" My mind happens
here at this kitchen table amid
these colored pencils (what a racket
they make when I feel among them
for the perfect black).

A termite without sin destroyed
the Choice of God at Lady Lake.
A local who reminds me my uncle
is a bleeding heart conservative
rewards the news-lady's
journalism-school compassion
with the usual remark.

Timothy Robbins

Today's my man's coldest day.
Bundled, we trudge up State Street
for a steaming cup. Mr. Greek
of Coney Island says, "Your man
walks like a kid." I suggest he look
at this sketch of Mike's eyes without lids.
"How well he'd guard your Parthenon!"

Hard Reach

Mike's hand foregoes the blanket's scant shelter.
Nocturnal creatures, their movements shaped by stealth,
are drawn from their home.
His fingers lead — obvious but worth stating,
digit's courage being seldom noticed.
It isn't just the blanket being dismissed. It's a whole staff:
sex-starved Westwood, Berkeley, San Francisco, Paris,
Ann Arbor, Milwaukee. It's not just his hand
landing on my tensed calf, petrifying my breath.
It's the buried hand that stabs the air in
the last seconds of a scary movie, the brown palm of the beautiful
Arab Lawrence loses to quicksand in David Lean's
grandest grandstand. The Blob (my brother made me see it)
starting no bigger than a ball of yarn, engulfed ever larger cats.
In the cameo-sized surrealist picture I painted on acid
it's the tulip sprouting from the floating kettle's spout.
It's desiccated stems, crazed as my raised legs,
scratching cinderblocks. I hear the hardness start
clear as ice starts on windows. All the world's diamonds
assume the toughest 6-sided stance.
God's tears are alchemized to mirrors. The spite between Father,
Son and Sprite enters eternal rigor mortis.
Our rigidities prove short-lived.

In the Air

I'm waiting for him to wake up.
I've been waiting as long as that
incurably healthy widow
across the street has
been waiting to give her
husband a piece of her mind.

Am I waiting for the resurrection
of the Jesus who laughed
breaking Sabbath rules,
the Light of the World
with chaff clinging to his robes —

or the mummy sealed in by,
not one, but a thousand stones?

It's a political question.
If it's the mummy that limps
down the hall and blindly
pours coffee, do I have
the capital to compel him

to the Grand Kite Launch in
Kennedy Park? Once there,

will the sight of wind-fighting
kites as colorful as me
with tails that could have
been cut from his wrapping,
shake him with their
obvious analogy?

Denny's Arbor Vitae

My Two Marriages

My first, like most, was a baby
husband. Lots of noise. No talk.
Red in the face if he
wasn't allowed to suck.
He treated me like any
first-time credit card holder
treats his credit.
I didn't mind. I amazed him
and with all his going out
and getting stuff and toting
it home and demonstrating
it breathlessly, he was
learning so fast it made us
both dizzy. Once or twice
I actually threw up.
My second was a born
parent. Always putting
his arm in front of me
when we were crossing
asphalt and figurative
streets. Lecturing me endlessly
on the dangers of bees
and millipedes and black
widows. Sometimes I caught
him looking at me with
wistful disappointment — I think

Timothy Robbins

because I didn't come from his
seed. One day my first
husband brought home an accident.
It blew up when he opened
the box. I would have been killed
too if I hadn't been standing
(I'd grown blasé) on
the other side of the room.
My second husband finally got
what he wanted.
Though I had come to him
unnaturally, Momotaro in his
peach, I was his true son.
Of course that meant no more
sex and separate rooms.

Denny's Arbor Vitae

No Day at the Beach

Kick a jetty. Be kidded by landmarks.
Egg on a pier that already cuts. Spy
on Tight Red Dress Lighthouse, wake
zone scrawled on its back, no wake
zone emblazoned on its front. Get out
and thrust when sand fine as dust holds
your tires. Shake sand from your socks.
Sweat drip after drip. Sidestep what
gulls drop, white as wings in the sun.
Wake as eventually you will (eventually
you won't). Take precautions for your
next back-float in shallows. In my
babbling you hear water and, fatally,
think I'll drown you. I was with you
so many times when you were going
too slow to steer that I learned to crave
speed as you craved it. We crawled
along coasts. We traced our rivers'
ready-made routes to encounters with
something native. Maybe it was love.
Maybe we infected and exploited it.
Our conscience made us stop trying
and we drifted back down to the sea.
We encountered something ancient.
Maybe trust. Maybe the hippo campus.
I heard neighing.

Timothy Robbins

Ode to a Boy from Hanoi

You have that determined
look of a child
with a grudge to protect.

I hope the grudge is me.

Day by day you sculpt in
my heart a new attitude
toward genius. From time to

time, in a blind rage,
I attack the statue.

I've spent hours on pews
and hours at bath houses
waiting for Pentecost.

Now it's sweet potato
fries for lunch while
the toaster oven ticks
like a bomb in an old movie

and a pigeon paces
looking as though it were
truly worried

and leaves two neat
little buds, pigeon turds
on the balcony rail.

Denny's Arbor Vitae

This is the time of year
when you slide the door
without knowing
whether you'll meet warmth
or chill. Chinese

sausages stacked on a
sheet of Bounty —
little logs for your own
little furnace.

Oh to live in film where
juxtaposition reigns more
eloquent than argument —
Fred Astaire singing,
"Just the way you look
tonight" while Ginger
washes her hair in an
unglamorous flat.

Reality and romance
meet and dance, swayingly,
to Jerome Kern's disarming
melody. Your knit cap,

too long for your head,
is rolled into fenders,
half-covering your ears.
Naked after rain seduced
the streets, you chased
your sisters with swear
words beyond your years.

Chicagos (for Mike)

According to a legend among my people, if
you surprise your reflection on the day after
Thanksgiving, you'll see behind you (like a
hairdresser waiting for your nod) the image
of unquestioning love. This is our fifth holiday
in Chicago. Our third since you quietly
dropped the pretense of reserving two beds. I
assume you know I'm proud. On the train
from Wisconsin we debate the question: Is
Kenosha a suburb of the Windy City? You say
yes, I say no. The train, a disciplined mediator,
withholds its opinion. Now, on a Sheraton king-
size, the movements of my legs are as effective
as the slicing of scissors guided by the fingers
of a Colonial silhouette-maker. Catnipped,
I purr with the Embassy Suite's three lifts
scooting up and down columns of night,
playing tag on Jacob's ladder. In the bathroom,
patiently, you wave the noisy blow-drier over
our wet shoes. We always get drenched in
this town. The rain makes you glisten like the
pavements you come from and soaks into
me like the fields around my birthplace.
Tomorrow morning at Ogilvie Transport Center,
excitedly, I'll explain my newest idea. An outer
Chicago, on which we leave no footprints.
An inner Chicago our purple soles beat.

Waiters

I waited till the train
unleashed
old folks with jet
propulsion walkers,
young toughs on
stately skateboards
and you, a
five-foot-six
juggernaut
rolling straighter
than fate. You startled
the frail as you strode
up behind them.
I wish you'd
seen me dancing,
freeing my feet
from the floor,
nudging a revolving
door in a city where
no one hurries.

Timothy Robbins

For Mike

When I look at his small
flooded body my hands like
Noah's birds
find no place to rest.

Denny's Arbor Vitae

Thanksgiving in Chicago

A non-Euclidian geography
explains how we traveled
together yet arrived at
different places. The Amtrak
lines were laid on a Möbius
strip and we boarded on
opposite sides. Only I see
cornices, flourishes, faces
sculpted on high, stone robes
with patinas of grime, grand,
grubby edifices reflected in
relentless mirrors of modernity.
I find on State Street the
essentials of a parade —
marchers and watchers
to stand and cheer. Some,
like me, discover this by
chance, amazed to find music
and dance rising from the
frigid pavement, amazed by
the reappearance of a
childhood self on a grownup's
shoulders. We slap our arms
for warmth and cheer marching
and mariachi bands, taiko
drummers, leaping Russians,

Timothy Robbins

and Harlem Globe Trotters.
Snug in the Hyatt Regency,
a mug of coffee at his elbow,
he marshals silent, elegant
equations. A gray river
pretends to empty into
end-of-the-earth fog:
the Chicago engineered
to flow against its nature.

Denny's Arbor Vitae

Today

He sleeps with one arm pressed to the sofa-back,
a model of nobility for continents
though no landmass, however slow its progress,
can imitate his grace.

Three of the other arm's fingers rest on his Adam's
apple, checking his pulse or the pulse of an
invisible necklace. His forgetfulness

is actually superstition.
The emptied packaging he leaves on the counter
is akin to the Prodigal Father's heart.

I love equanimity for not deserting my body.
I love it almost as much as I love him.

I don't get hard in the presence of other men anymore.
The people who killed Alan Turing
would say I'm cured.

The half-eaten apple waits on the curb
ready to talk to the cops.
For a second, Alan mistakes the paramedic
for a prince.

Must be a holiday. The blind magician
doesn't miss a trick. The deaf contralto is
never off key. The Indian husband is in
traditional garb — painful white from neck to ankle —
impeccable as my dad's Cadillac right after he
washed it back in the 70s when he
really didn't have the time.

First warm wind. Still the cold milk carton handle
bites my curled fingers. Alternating hands
add rhythm to my parade past the dandelions,
whom I greet wondering which generation they are.

There's something seriously depraved about
their numerous enemies.
About this, sleeping or waking, we agree.

Stuck

I'm stuck with this consolation:
You whip up a skillet of chicken curry.
You eradicate the microbe colony
in the sink. You ignore everyone but me,
your widow's mite more beneficial to your
Karma than a thousand Sutras.
The papers I threw at the 'possum in
the dumpster by the light of the last
super moon were prayers to that half of
the Prime Mover I was born to worship
and accuse. I sat down on the first stone
that would sit still for me and started
bargaining for balls full of flightless
birds. You're not that over-imaginative
simpleton. You don't actually make
me dizzy. No man ever has. I thought
one did once but now I know that was really
the coke he shot into the crook of my arm.
Most people don't know what painlessness is.
None knows how I feel licking
your lips as you scan a night sky
for an enlightened satellite.

Skater

Passengers

Letter to Gregg

Through the muffle of the snow I hear a lost bird sing.
How tired he is of winter and how he dreams of spring.
You and I stretched out on a mattress from the street.
The moon prayed like a mad woman for our bodies to meet.
We lay on a moonstruck mattress through all the winter cold.
We watched like mad children to see if our vows would hold.
Do you remember how Peter danced with a blind cigarette?
Ashes on his pajama shirt, a sight I'll never forget.

Ah beneath the winter stars, the first joint that we shared.
I see its riddle when I look up just as we wrote it there.
Handsome in your coat of down and your curls of jet.
Deep the drag you took upon a bitter cigarette.
One hand rested on my head that rested on your chest.
You exhaled without a cough and said your life was blessed.
 Do you remember how Peter danced, a bottle clinched in his fist?
Wine splattered on the rug. He danced a blind man's twist.

Denny's Arbor Vitae

We lived on T.S. Eliot, Williams, James and Joyce.
We blended Dylan and the Dead into a single voice.
We pondered by secret candlelight in a midnight hush
mysteries of religions that never belonged to us.
From remains of our past loves and clods of holy land
we made ourselves a golem to serve us on command.
Do you remember how Peter danced, a foreign song on his lips,
seeking that never died on his fingertips?

A letter stained with coffee and still a lost bird sings,
mingling with his prophecies his faith in earthly things.
This is no real letter, it bears no real address.
It's a Torah. It's a Gospel. It speaks of righteousness.
Righteousness that in the past spoke through word and deed.
Righteousness that now is lost and scattered like our seed.
Do you remember how Peter danced as the light was growing dim?
Day and night, dark and light, all the same to him.

The Way of Tim Ash

You have a way of appearing, the chorus in
a Satyr Play. The night before my hernia repair
you look better than you have in years. Your
cheeks imply you've renounced fasting.
You look as resilient as you did when we
kissed in Dunn Meadow. In the Trojan Horse
we kiss the baklava. Like president and
governor, post-hurricane, we tour undergrad
shelters. The hut where a tree sowed persimmons
among gravel, the hovel where roaches
drove household gods from the oven, a night
sky, somehow still there, slowed down by
airy-headed fire balloons. Talking all the while
like years ago when I thought we were falling
in love. You preach the virtues of polygamy —
poly-fidelity you call it — and communal
child-rearing. You tell me you still sleep
with Eddie. (He picked you up the summer
you hitchhiked to Vancouver. You both
pretended it was a rescue.) What am I thinking
through all this? What am I supposed to
think when you ask to crash here? You have
this way of showing up like the stranger in a
Jewish tale appearing to the bride on the eve
of her wedding. She can't tell the angel from

Denny's Arbor Vitae

the demon unless she un-shoes him and checks
for hooves. I make up the hideaway for you.
Leaning on a pillow, you read me a poem
by Shelley. I read Matthew Arnold. In the
middle of the night the white strip of bed
beckons like a ledge. I lie against your
back growing stiff-necked and hungry knowing
I can't eat till after the operation. I hear voices
whisper, "Love, let's be false to each other."

Tannenbaum

Arbor vitae outside a Denney's window.
Across the parking lot
white pines fanning high in the air.
In front of the Motor Lodge
three cedars like Christmas trees
stripped of their rank.
Tannenbaum piped into the dining room

The town seems confused
with the students gone.

In the first scare after the test results
you talked of changing your life.
No more cigarettes. No more beer.
No more days when you just forget to eat.
No more euchre till four in the morning,
making love till six,
snatching two hours of sleep
before feeling your way to class.

You wanted to decorate your crib for Christmas.
A tree bigger than childhood,
bulbs of every color, lights
flashing like a migraine.
The florist thought I was crazy
when I asked for the tree of life.

Denny's Arbor Vitae

This morning I'm breakfasting alone.
The sunshine bleeds like the words of Jesus
in a red letter edition.
You are in Gary by now.
For the first time in your life
you don't feel safe in your mother's home.
The danger is in your blood.
No amount of prayer, no crib, no cross
will change you to the rose e'er blooming.

Marc

1.
I don't remember why we went
to the hospital that day. Blood work?
To report on negotiations between
your body and the latest drug?
To distract a fellow patient or flirt
with a Filipino orderly? I remember
being impressed how you navigated
the halls, not even glancing at the
colored lines, those rainbow veins.
While I was lost, as in a dream house
with infinitely propagating rooms, you
needed neither crumbs nor stones
nor Ariadne's string.

2.
Platonic is my word for you.
We never so much as danced.
Never troubled each other's desires.
And you were the the incorrigible
academic, constructing dialogues,
braving your way through metaphoric
caves. You even had Plato's build,
that bullish torso, so the day your
brother led a frail old man into
the museum, holding him by the
arm, I didn't know it was you till
you spoke.

3.
I'm glad there's no afterlife. I hate
to think of all those pills in opaque
plastic cups, and you looking down
in envy, rage or disgust as I take my
nightly dose.

4.
You joked that you were majoring
in Plague Studies
and your new mentor was Saint
Roch. Your account was so vivid,
I couldn't get it out of my head
for weeks. The first
appearance of the dog,
the bread soggy with its saliva.
The dog's tongue closing
wounds, the opposite of Thomas's
finger. The dream of the dog's
kiss, the fevered pant on the
face. Days when the saint
wished the dog would
kill him. Hours he cursed the
poor who fed him
nothing but the disease.

5.
You talked right up to the end,
speaking proudly of John as
though he was to be a patriot's
widow, fussing about the people
gathered around your bed,
worrying about the structure
you had made. I wish you
could see us now and be relieved
by structure's tendency to decay.

Essay

I can only approximate his Malay
name. Can't picture the sturdy
Mohammedan face he rested on
classmates' shoulders. The heat
must have felt immature, amateurish.
Indiana was a new country for him,
as teaching was for me. He wrote
simply, longingly of a hairdresser's
half-repressed smile, of her nails on
his scalp making the locks' black
stingray undulate in the watery sink.
His lids met like fingertips
extinguishing a flame.

What We Know

The mango's a red dawn whose diffuse
border gently burns, fades into green
sky. The mango is sunset bleeding into
grass. Dulce brings me a fine mango
five mornings a week. I don't know if
students do this in her country or if
she heard about the teacher's apple and
chooses to give it a personal, a national
touch. She doesn't know I have a husband,
but she knows I've never had a wife, and
maybe guesses the rest. She doesn't know
why I go to the hospital. She knows I
never specify and maybe that's enough.
I know she has two boys — Juan and
Henry (never Enrique) and I know they
live with her mother-in-law but not her
husband. I know mornings when Saudis,
Malians, and her fellows Hondurans
complain of the Michigan cold, her smile
is as tropical as her offering, her laughter
as generous as the sun is stinting. Today
I learned from Grisdie, her husband was
shot one evening defending the family
carwash.

Nostalgia

After he left the hospital he
disappeared — like a war criminal.
Two years later, in the middle
of laundry, a phone call from Kentucky.
"Don't you remember us?"
I remember reading about us
between Cher's anorexia and
a ten-year-old mother.
I remember the first week you wanted
to marry me. I gave the same vows
I pledged the neighbor girl when I was six.
I remember sickness.
Spoon-feeding each other cough syrup.
The hellish nights you
forgot your antidepressants.
The day you rushed to the emergency
room with a cold and demanded
a second opinion...
"Don't you remember the sex?"
I remember your roommate.
You said her boyfriend was so big
they had to use the backdoor and
it was getting wide as a garage.
I remember your high school buddy.
We both wanted him so badly we
got drunk and passed out in separate rooms...
"Don't you remember *our* love-making?"
I remember listening once.
It was like neighbor's moans
rising through vents.

Chantel Two Days Before Halloween

Reading a smile, interpreting a poem with nothing to go on but the font.
"What are you so happy about?"
He stomps down the stairs and struggles into loafers
while I step lightly behind.
"Remember the custodian at the Traymore who strutted standing still?"

I have no furrier. Chantel is my courier.
A crocheted Tam o' shanter
(she delivers monthly meds and banter) is crushed on her head.
Mike is my worrier but Chantel is my courier.
Cat's eye specs curl at her temples in twenty-sixteen.
Her mouth is yellower than Ringo's submarine.
Her ringtone on my phone is "The Ride of the Valkyries."
No one is Valkyrier than she.
When the virus hears the Wagnerian fanfare,
its sky breaks out in choppers.
Martin Sheen squats in the backseat of the Love Bug she
drives in twenty-sixteen. No, it's her four-year-old son
who will catapult from the catbird seat
and rush to Mama's knees if she seems
about to sneeze in the direction of my open door.
"Abandonment issues" I opine and she agrees.

He was hungry-crabby from waiting all day.
When the doorbell finally rang,
I was listening to Leon Redbone, watching Basil Rathbone dangle
from the ceiling, handcuffed to a pipe.
Why was I so happy?
The bite-size Snickers treat did the trick. The tot
stepped from behind his mother who till that moment
was his totem and pillar. "What do you say?" she prompted.

Charla and the Traveler

I exchanged pleasantries with an extraterrestrial at an art fair. I was looking up at a mobile attached to a street lamp, reaching down not quite touching me. "A shame there's not a sigh of wind today," the alien said, suddenly beside me. "A good breeze would bring that piece to life." "Or turn it into a machine without purpose." The other fair-goers were oblivious. Maybe noticing that most of the art fair was not art, they'd stopped categorizing. I spotted him because he fit a description Charla Mehas gave me when she was thirty and I was sixteen. "Both he and she and neither, it visits at the new moon. Its face stops at my bedroom window. Its tentacles, a different number every visit, rush at me like happy children that climb on adults with no sense of how they might hurt or excite us. I tickle them until they flee screaming or lay panting beside the bed." She was the mother my mother feared I wanted. Summer slow, thorough,

hot like the Amish that sometimes
nodded from their buggies and other
times concentrated straight ahead in
solidarity with their horses. Her
husband Bill was Zorba the Greek
wrapped in a Union agitator, wrapped
in a train engineer. I seldom heard him
speak — and wondered if his utterances
actually came from his curly black beard.
Their kids were Saffron, Savannah,
Sage and Slade. They scraped by
in a house where yellow was mellow,
brown got flushed down and an old
dentist's chair as sturdy as the past
was the only living room furniture.
They gave parties where clothes
were not on the guest list and party
favors included tiny paper wafers.
Something about her sang, "Come
out to me! Let me be the rehearsal
for your mom and dad, the foundation
on which you'll raise a skyscraper
of acceptance."

Engagement

Gregg strikes guitar strings
like beating a snare.
High E will snap. It will startle
and the relaxed string
will flop till anthem's end.
 Everything takes part in the
acoustics. His shaking Hebraic
curls. Frayed threads of Levi
cutoffs (white cornsilk) on
tensed thighs. The closet-ness
of a quad room. The clumsy
rhythm that belies a
furniture-mover's grace.
"Four Dead in Oh High Oh."
A stress pattern foreign to
English, for all I know, true
to Iroquoian for "Good
River." I'm not thinking
about Kent Stat. When he
stretches on his stomach, dead
to the world, I'll incarnate
the Pulitzer winner: a silent
scream, one knee down,
an outstretched hand built
to hold a box pierced by a ring.

Francele

The Women

Miss Taylor's mouth intense as
paraffin lips we chewed at Halloween.
Miss Taylor puckering at sopranos
and tenors with her impartial, arch
"Ah-ha!"
I cast her first in my remake
of the Cukor classic,
savoring yesteryear's waxy flavor.
Mouth so red, black and white
can't dim it.
Breasts as load-bearing
as a forklift's tongs.
Baton more awe-inspiring
than a judge's gavel.
How she waved it at mothers
who wanted to stop Ken and me from
singing "Imagine" in the high school
auditorium.
I dedicate this film to Dad,
envier of my friendships with women.
Even his wife of 52 years —
he can't make her laugh as I can.
Nor does he relish as I relish
her genius for portmanteau.
("This medicine makes me *droggy.*"
"Your cousin hated his *stinch*
in the Army.")
All night long in a tent before his
sad hungry eyes I flaunt them.
Stephanie, who put my brother and me
in her outgrown dresses.

In the picture,
Bruce is sulky. I grin like a tipsy
birthday gift.
Suzanne, who stepped out of the
Leonard Cohen song.
Nell (her dad called her the poor man's
Streisand). She quelled a fight
by putting her arm around one of the
frat boys' shoulders.
Beth, my homemade sister who laughed,
relieved as a blister
when I came out in her
living room. Shelley, whose first time
was backstage at the Bean Blossom
Festival with a mandolinist whose
fingers worked wonders on
the narrowest frets.
Angela, who swapped with me tales
from Bullwinkle's
(the gay and lesbian bar, so named
for having been a Moose lodge).
I couldn't picture myself between her
thighs, but I was in love with
her olive green irises. Judy,
who lost the distinction between her
husband and his
meat and potatoes. Nadine
who sparkled with the glitterati in a
Belle Époque flat
above the Seine.
A middle-aged sparrow who divorced
her dream-crushing hubby.

Denny's Arbor Vitae

A middle aged vulture who lived to
break the spell a witch
had laid on her ex-spouse.
Both claimed their happiness was yet
to come. I think the
sparrow was right. Sometimes I think
I'd be happiest in this
movie where the men are
kept offstage. But then, who can say?

Train

Nothing happens on this train. We should be thankful for this. This train's bound for nowhere. Give thanks for that too.

We jog up Madison Street. Luggage slows our pace. We open our coats and unwind our scarfs.

Winter air mugs us. Ogilvie Station. I hope for guys to ogle on the train (word games make journeys bearable — ask Odysseus). Preferably they'll be snoozing so I can ogle at my leisure. With impunity. We're heading for a new life, une nouvelle vie, where you'll vie for tenure, for harmless anorexia, for an apotheosis of superstition, for a privacy so complete even you won't know our address. I will vie in my own small way for a shareable happiness.

The invisible hand of commerce stocks the seats with commuters. Each, via boarding rituals, reveals some secret. Answering my prayers, five young sailors, snug in pea coats, collars turned up like 18th century capes, on their way to Station Great Lakes, flop into their seats and start to gossip.

Pulling from oily dark
    new life suicide paradise
        new life suicide paradise
            new life suicide paradise
                to dingy light,
                    every joint of the train jitters.

All trains hurtle toward the future on rails joined by ties that might as well be corpses. They ignore or stop impatiently at invocations of my past. Nothing happens. No Aryan

Nation Jihadist with boxcutters tucked into his belt. No rambunctiously dressed fans off to shine Lady Gaga's boots.

Approaching Evanston, where Gregg learned to beat the truth out of a guitar. Where his green boy-flesh gradually acquired a mango blush. Where his parents sold their house and he rescued the mezuzah and gave it to me. Inside, a piece of paper rolled like a joint bore witness to our Undergraduate chosen people entanglement. Departing Kenilworth. A paperback for Christmas when I was 15. Delusions of Pre-Raphaelites and doomed hushed weddings and studly blonds riding behind long pointy lances (on se lance vers une vie de nouveautés). Approaching Raven's Wood. Raven, the self-inflicted name of the first man who persuaded me to love the shock of raven skin against my pallor.

After Highwood we try a game of Hangman using names of people who were hanged but shouldn't have been and people we'd like to see hanged. Then a game of Abstraction Alphabet. Absolution. Atman. Bounty. Brevity. Charm. Credulity...Xenophobia, Xerox-ability, Yin, Yang (Yahwism as an alternate), Zoology, Zeal. We reminiscence about our apartment hunt, the cabbie that was supposed to pick us up early Sunday morning but never showed up and the night clerk at the motel who gave us a lift to the station although it was against regulations. Best part of that trip was the agents, some trying to figure out if we were a couple, some assuming we were.

We are Shakyamuni
riding a lotus.
No part of us touches ground.
An incomplete art
completes us.

And signs shout from Turret's Towers: SELF STORAGE
KNOW YOUR ENEMY LET'S WORK TOGETHER
FULFILL YOUR DREAM. Hubbard's Wood makes me
think of the kid who carried me onto a stage — Jim laying
Tom Sawyer on Aunt Sally's settee.

Tool and Dye Maker

Strasbourg Gang

Straight guys of my twenties
don't interest me.
If cops accused me of caring,
cops'd be unable to show
motive or opportunity.

Chris Robinson was last
spotted, the last human
stranded on the seven
hills of Cincinnati. Mostly
I liked his taste for zaftig

women. Good-looking as
he was, undervalued as they
are, he must have been
rolling in bliss all these
years. But then, that just

shows how impoverished my
notions of happiness are.
Ted Dagnese was last seen
on the corner of Market
and Van Ness, saying my

name, an amazed question.
Come to think, he was
well set up too, his attraction
for mean-looking cover girls
being no match for his

Timothy Robbins

love of classical music.
Even a third-chair cellist
could easily draw him like
a bow across her strings.
It's Jim I'd worry about if

I worried. Politics was his
shield against loneliness.
Lord, the senators he could
rattle off, the congressional
debates he could quote from.

And the newspapers he
consumed! Fifty a day,
a legend like Balzac's cups,
but with a bean or two of
truth. I imagine his suffering

over the state of the nation
and yes, I'd relieve him
of it if I could. But it's not like
this deletable writing or the
disposable photo that prompted it.

Chris and I, our sharp profiles
framing Birgit, (his confidant
and unrequited crush) —
her soft round face softened
even further by

that property of the camera,
that singularity of focus that
softens the metal, the escalator,
the wall and ceiling glass of
the terminal behind us.

Sandra's Poem

Umbrellas hang from an atrium ceiling,
someone's idea of art.
Why do I think of you? Because we are
an art project of Providence?
Is it just that I know this misuse of
brollies would amuse you?
Or that you'd snort at my invocation
of an unseen provider?
Autumn in Brazil while it's spring here
is the heart of the yin-yang
that conceived us. I'm
listening to music you send and wishing
I could wink like a Paulistano.
Such a wink in the mirror would tumble
me back in love with myself. "If,"
you scold, "Americanos hadn't hauled
the Greek Gods before the WTO…"
"they would stretch our limbs on the rack,
crack our skin to bark
and plant us as willows." "What is
this *willow*?" And after checking your
translator, "*Que nojo*! Why you make
me this pathetic tree?"
"We'll dip our branches into the stream
and tickle bored fish when
they tire of feeling scaly."
"*Garoto tolo*, let the fish tickle us!"
"Feisty sister, what matters it
so long as meaning is tickled from the
meaningless?"

The Portrait

The precocity of a 16-year old former
wrestler is clear in each pencil stroke —
and discouraging in the overall effect.
Discouraging to me, the one who started
him drawing. He repaid my envy with
a 30x28 inch tribute. It hung
above my parents' sideboard for 36 years
waiting for me to see he had depicted the
blend of artistic imp and brainy Osmond
I wanted to be. This was my outer face
turned on a lathe like a coat stand. Not
the acne desert I wandered chilly as the
frozen nitrogen the dermatologist
spritzed on my skin. I think of my father,
whose embrace was never that cold —
not an Indiana winter, but not tropical either.
Except for times he caught my
twelve-year-old face in his tool-hardened
hands and with manipulations fit to free
a tick, thumb-nail a flea or repair a tiny
engine, he eased the first blackheads
from my cheeks.

The Messenger

A small airplane, mowing Sunday sky,
stutters past, fatuous in its love for the local.

The invisible roars by, leans into the turn,
spills a bee from the sidecar. The biker

leans into goggles, leans into hard air,
shouts and fails to notice. The bee staggers

and I recall a cousin of his my paintbrush
hung from acrylic wings. It was a yellow

bee and it hung in silver ether. Small for a
canvas, big for a bumble — exaggerated

as the buzzer in the shed where my brother
locked me as a boy. A blind and angry bee

that bashed against the walls. I packed the
canvas board in bubble-wrap and shipped

it to Tom. Maybe he looks at it rapturously.
This wouldn't be odd for a man who speaks

odes over poppy fields and spends New
Year's Eves in the Santa Monica hills.

Timothy Robbins

The bee staggers and I remember the time
my back betrayed me. I crawled to the parking

lot and into Tom's car, and he drove me to
the ER where a shot of morphine sent me

hurtling from hallucination's gurney. Tom,
is this bee your reminder that Westwood's

three hours away as the plane flies? And I
owe you a long jaw at the Jamba Juice?

Kotaro

Shut the windows on the Santa Anas
and I'll free your false blond locks.
Why do you trust my razor on your scalp
but not my head in you lap?
I too am ambivalent aout our intimacy, how
it bloomed in exposed places: on the
verandah of Border's cafe, at parties that
filled friends' apartments then
spilled into shared hallways, in dim pet
stores where we imitated the mouthings of
luminous fish, on Santa Barbara's white
sands where walking on your hands turned
the beach upside-down. We talked of
thwarted recoveries. You were squirming
in a toxic romance. I was straining toward
monogamy. You were giving up pot. I was
renouncing Tina. We ignored the healings
that worked: the smelly lump
removed from my forearm, the hernia repair
that turned laughter into torture,
the hole in your heel from the night you went
berserk in a parking garage, egged on
by your own bellowing, leaping like a
springbok till stopped by a traffic spike.
These successes belonged to doctors and
our unthinking bodies.
Your bandages come off. We wander
into a Jewish carpet shop on Westwood with
Farsi script on the windows. Slyly,
we touch the silken rugs. Side by side
in front of my stunted TV we observe

the mother in *Tampopo* serve her family
with her last impetus, hear the father
shout at the children to eat, eat every bite
before she and the food grow cold.
We hear the quarrelsome cooks in *Akahige*
call the urchin thief's name down the well.
Such a pain he'd been. Nothing less than
his death could have made them submit
to his grin or admit he had a soul worth
calling home. In *Gohatto* we watch the
soulless beauty of a young samurai bring
murder to the ranks of the Shinsengumi.
Your tonsured head doesn't make you
Gautama. Shorn locks don't weaken you.
No sympathetic magic imprisons you
when I seal your clippings in a box that
was a Whitman's sampler.

Kazu

I wish we'd kept in touch. I want to
tell you I'm rereading the Murakami
novel. I want to convince you of the affection
I feel for a minor character, the caretaker who
minds the power station and collects
musical instruments for their shapes as
I collect shapes for their pitch. I say 'reread.'
Actually I'm listening to an audio book.
I didn't love the caretaker when he was mute.
I've fallen for him now for the narrator's
voice like a wind from a world that has only
one wind.

I pray your kickboxing is still so
precise it's not violent — pray you're still
a percussionist not a pugilist in the ring.
I loved the narrow forehead you would
have hid. Imagine a pregnant girl who
doesn't know what's happening to her body
or how it came about. Your relation to your
beauty is that girl's relation
to her gestating heir.

John

Film student, woodsman, carpenter.
Hair like curls from a plainer.
Eyes that jumped as in REM sleep.

The vice-grip of his hands,
the stretching of his arms
showed the depth of his woodcraft

even when he was aiming
a camera, stirring a pot,
soaping his body or rinsing his locks.

He was unabashed in the showers
like a toddler, pre-apple Adam,
Methuselah shuffling to his
locker at the Y.

He steered his pickup with
his left palm. His right hand,
like pollen, settled on mine.

He took me to auctions, bought me
weird props. A bronze
ashtray shaped like an oak leaf.

Denny's Arbor Vitae

A doctor's bag, musty as a basement.
A convex lens, wide as his handspan,
filched from the AV department.

I turned that lens into a gem
bright as stones he gave his girl.
It un-blurred his plot the night
he motioned me to climb up
and burrow under their quilt.

Joel

You were my first J.W. I met
you around the time Prince died.
Were it not for you I would
have been snottier about the
metrosexual musician's conversion.
You were the first that wasn't
on my threshold polite as a
vampire, hoping to be let in,
hoping I'd swap "All Along the
Watchtower" for "The Watchtower"
point blank. I liked the funny
stories about your sinful past.
The way you always came to
class early with a question in
your shirt pocket.
Your soft spoken-ness
(natural or the result of
much whispered prayer?)
I'm writing this with the pen
you gave me: a silhouette of
Christ and the two thieves,
the name of your church
(La Hermosa) and the address
you suppose I will need. Two
moments flank me like those
robbers. Your father-in-law's

Denny's Arbor Vitae

heart surgery and how his wife
monitored the procedure online
with composure, we agreed,
beyond our understanding.
The rolling of your eyes (not
like El Greco's heaven-gazing
saints) when one of your classmates
told us his husband had given
him a Benz for his birthday.
I wanted the gall to make that
eight-inch incision, to saw through
the breastbone, letting in
unwelcome light.

Harry's Poem

Before I tell the dream: I came across a
bogus website

that claimed my mother's name is American
for "Famous Elf."

I decided the resemblance between Harry
Kirshner (my first art tutor)

and Hare Krishna (my first Asian Christ)
was no accident.

I say Harry/Hare means "one who
barbers and paints with awkward affection."

I say Kirshner/Krishna, from an Indo-
European root for reach, means

"one whose arms never stop growing."
A bus or train shakes Lan and me

like martinis that will be drunk by martini
connoisseurs. My legs are

a lawn chair that hasn't been opened in
years. When I restore their legginess,

I discover Harry one seat behind ours, his
legs crossed at the ankles

Denny's Arbor Vitae

à la Lana Turner at the Top Hat Café or
Schwab's Drugstore.

He joins us in what suddenly becomes a
diner booth, the transition

as surprising as the expected change
from boy to youth. I ask where he's going.

"To see a retrospective of a pioneering
plastic surgeon."

The jerking of the diner makes me spill
the martinis. Harry looks relieved.

A porter or waiter appears with a stack
of paintings done when I was ten

and unceremoniously pours them onto the
table. "Might it be one of these?"

Harry says what he's looking forward
to most at the exhibition

is Vitruvian Man trapped like John
Travolta in

"The Boy in the Plastic Bubble." I
think about the absence

of the dream world from most of the
world's paintings

and from all philosophy before Freud;
about the insanity that ensues

when REM sleep is repeatedly
disturbed; about what would return if

all lifelike pictures were buried
or burned.

The Brothers

1.
We've been forced out of our first hiding place --
Sepulveda in the roaring shadow of the 405,
where Hamburger Heaven barely lights the sidewalk,
the blue awning newsstand exposes Hillary Clinton and
her extraterrestrial baby, and a woman in a dirty
coat feeds feral kittens in the strip of grass
beside the overpass. It wasn't the Northridge
quake that dislodged us. It wasn't the unaccustomed
stars like a thousand prying eyes spying on us when the
electricity was cut. It was your courage. It was
faith that your parents were filled with Jesus's love, not
Christ's condemnation. Now as I drive this rented
car alone, my throat is sore as though I've been face-
fucked by Yahweh. My sinuses are blocked as though
I were breathing nose-down in a pillow.

2.
And Now they are taking us in. They are redeeming
the sin of Sodom. Giotto is painting them, chipping
away their gilding, returning icons to living flesh.
They serve in lazar houses. They dance in the Porziuncola.
They fill their three-story Victorian with bearded Welsh
priests. They board rent boys from the streets, lodging them
for free in rent-controlled flats. Brother Robert,
who eats curry till his eye bags twitch, stuffs us with

boiled roots. Brother Justice, who sucks cigars
on the stoop, stores our luggage in a room whose books
truly make a narrow path to his cot. Brother Jim, who grinds
his teeth, enacting Luke 13:28, keeps us awake at night.
Eighty years old, Brother Leo warns us of the wicked
"Bishop of Rome," and nods off in front of *"Are You
Being Served?"* On the flood-lit court across the street
a young man's slicing return leaves us and Brother
Otis breathless. The night air, vinegary from apples
rotting in the neighbors' yard, inspires Brother Antonio
to harvest and can these Edenic Jonathans.

For Nell

My first — my virgin surgery you might say —
was a hernia repair, sewing shut a membrane
that had been ripped open. In that sense the
opposite of first coitus. You drove me to the
hospital. Napped in the waiting room. Nursed
me at your parents' house while they were
vacationing in Mexico. Watched a Hitchcock
marathon as I drifted in and out of anesthesia
feeling a lot like Jimmy Stewart in Vertigo. I
fretted about the tarantula in a terrarium in your
father's room. Through a fog of deadened pain,
I heard your explanation of how Hitch got Cary
Grant to look so scared by running a spider across
his arachnophobic hand. The second surgery lifted
a lump from my breast — gynecomastia, which has
nothing to do with being transgender but seemed
the appropriate ailment for a total bottom like me.
Spotting you in the waiting room, the doctor wanted
to know if you were my wife. "No, that's my bosom
buddy," I quipped. I don't think he got the joke.

Farewell

Farewell and my apologies to the creature in the dumpster.
I know I startled you as much as you startled me.
Farewell to a Wolverine in a pork pie hat
whistling the opening bars of the New World Symphony.
To a skirted retro-hippie teetering on an antique bike a shade
of peach to make the Peach God weep. To a gopher on State Street
shaking its rump as it waddled into a thicket. To a deer
stock still, tensed to leap at the sound of human step.
To the Huron that attracted a plenary of species
right outside our balcony. To the black squirrels and skyscraper
trees of Eberwhite Wood — survivors of a primeval solitude,
even greater survivors than me. To Dave at the White Market.
To his sad vegetables, his day-old donuts, his friendly sagging face.
He too was a survivor. To Methodist children making a jolly game
of raking while their parents stood by looking stern. To
priests wading through magnolia petals beside
Thomas the Apostle. To lonely men cruising Mason Hall.
To the Rudolph Wurlitzer in the Michigan Theater
accompanying Lon Chaney's 1925 Phantom of the Opera.
To my classroom windows above the marquee. To Sandra,
who (very much against her will) rode to school
on the back of her daughter's motorbike. As though
any Brazilian mother needed a pretext to wrap
her arms around her daughter and hold on tight. Especially
if that daughter's a gay soldier training for the FBI.

Denny's Arbor Vitae

To Father Nabil, a Lebanese Maronite with powers of forgiveness and flirtation deep as the roots of his homeland's cedars. To Charlie, who never spoke of the family he lost when Burma became Myanmar, who brought from his garden herbs and a squash of Earth's deepest green. To the notary public in the bike shop of all places with a jealous chihuahua nipping at her heels as she signed and sealed our affidavit of Domestic Partnership.

Kinatro's lucky disaster

Publishing Credits

"Infancy of Recording" was first published in *Hanging Loose* 102.

"Isometrics" was first published in Hanging Loose 82.

"It" was first published in *American Chordata*, Issue Four, Fall 2016.

"The Night Mom Chased a Thief" was first published in *Hanging Loose* 101.

"Breaking the Diaries" was first published in *Slant*, Summer 2017.

"Weddings" was first published in *Main Street Rag*, Volume 21 Summer 2016.

"Raphael" was first published in *Adelaide Literary Magazine*, March 2017.

"Foundation" was first published in *Hanging Loose* 106.

"Trails" was first published in *Hanging Loose* 104.

"Night Visitors" was first published in *Hanging Loose* 103.

"Bowing" was first published in *Cactus Heart* 15.

"Chuang Tzu's Butterfly" was first published in *Off The Coast*, Spring 2016.

"The Cut" was first published in *The Opiate*, May 2017.

"Diagnosed" was first published in *The Tishman Review* Volume 2, Issue 4, October 2016.

"Fault Lines" was first published in *Main Street Rag*, Volume 21 Number 2 Spring 2016.

"Sal Mineo" was first published in *Off The Coast*, Fall 2015.

"How You Came to Me" was first published in *Hanging Loose* 108.

"Marriage" was first published in *Hanging Loose* 80.

"You are Sitting at the Table" was first published in *Two Thirds North* 2016.

"The Way of Tim Ash" was first published in *Adelaide Literary Magazine*, March 2017.

"Tannenbaum" was first published in *Tipton Poetry Journal*, Spring 2016.

"Marc" was first published in *Rock and Sling* 2017.

"Essay" was first published in *Adelaide Literary Magazine*, June 2017.

"Nostalgia" was first published in *Hanging Loose* 56.

"The Brothers" was first published in *Hanging Loose* 106.

"Farewell" was first published in *The Sow's Ear*, Volume 26, Number 3, Winter 2017.

About the Author

Timothy Robbins teaches ESL and does freelance translation in Wisconsin. He has a BA in French and an MA in Applied Linguistics from Indiana University. He has been a regular contributor to *"Hanging Loose"* since 1978. His poems have also appeared in *Adelaide Literary Magazine, Three New Poets, The James White Review, Slant, Main Street Rag, Two Thirds North, The Pinyon Review, Wisconsin Review*, and others. *Denny's Arbor Vitae* is his first published book of poetry.

Timothy Robbins

Denny's Arbor Vitae

www.ingramcontent.com/pod-product-compliance
Lightning Source LLC
Chambersburg PA
CBHW020614300426
44113CB00007B/636